THE
REMITTANCE
MAN

KENNY WARD

Paperback: 978-1-967820-60-3
eBook: 978-1-967820-61-0
Library of Congress Control Number: 2025910201

This is a work of nonfiction.

Ordering Information:

Prime Seven Media
518 Landmann St.
Tomah City, WI 54660

Printed in the United States of America

TABLE OF
CONTENTS

FOREWORD.

These events took place over thirty years ago. The anecdotes of 'George' are true. Being so long ago, I did not remember all the names of the Character, so I took the liberty of making them up. Some of the people mentioned are also fictitious. If anyone recognizes themselves, please excuse the name.

I have also had to streamline the Characters for the sake of the story. I have omitted some families that were very kind to me while I was there, for example the Adams' in Salisbury and my good friend Brian Hodgson.

I have deliberately left out references to the Political situation at the time.

This book is not about Religion, Politics or Race. It is about a young man who spent three years in a Police Force, and his experiences there.

THE START
OF IT ALL.

'KEEP FORMATION and paddle across the lake towards the cameras' yelled the Instructor at the top of his voice. A section of 6 young men were canoeing across a Welsh lake in the Snowdonia National Park. They were part of an Outward Bound Course up from London. The Instructor has his own canoe at the back, and really needed to shout, because the gale winds blowing down the lake, were wiping his words away. The lake surface had chopped up quite a bit, so the K 2 wooden canoes were difficult to handle. With their assortment of paddlers pulling hard towards the eastern side of the lake, the cameras rolling. Sure enough, one guy went in. They had all done B.C. U. (British Canoe Union) course in Ham, London before coming here so they knew what to do. The Instructors went to help him, but their chances of finishing up on the finished film, had diminished.

Pathe New were doing an 'Easter Activity' piece, showing how young men and women spend their Easter Holiday. This was part of the piece. Their chances of 15 minutes of fame now may have been reduced, by their weakest link taking an early dive. The piece did show however, but no names were mentioned.

George Shipman, the designated leader of the group pulled his craft up onto the bank of the lake. He was five feet eleven inches, broad shoulders and strong build, from playing Rugby and soccer, for various amateur teams. He swam, loved Cricket and generally could get by, in any ball sport. Sandy hair, blue/green eyes, a good jaw line and broad forehead, he didn't shirk from taking responsibilities, but he didn't seek them out either.

"That's it for the day lads' Shouts Jack Broad, the Instructor, an Ex-marine P.T.I. six feet three inches tall, solidly built with a balding head, and square jaw, 'Get the canoes back on the trailer, and we'll go back to base camp'. George and his pal, Mike Seely grabbed their two canoes. Mike in front, one prow in his left hand one in the right. Similarly at the back, a stern in each hand George lifted up. Off towards the trailer they went. The rest of the team took their own.

When all was sorted out, Jack Broad drove the Land-Rover and trailer to a group of cottages, about 4 miles away over the dirt tracks, which was base camp. The cottages had been specially renovated to accommodate suck groups. Serious climbers and trekkers used the facilities.

Set in a background of the glorious Welsh mountains, accessed by trails, and tracks. Coarse grass and shrubs survived up here naturally, Humans just visited.

George and Mike had teamed up, as both were a shade older than the others and a bit more grown up. They were 18, to the other 16-17 but then the difference was quite noticeable, in many ways of maturing and developing young men.

"That's back to London tomorrow then' said Mike, 'What are you going to do then?'

'I've got another Brewery Course to go on, but I am not looking forward to it really, I would love to travel a bit and get away, but dad wants me to take over from Him, but he's got years ahead on him yet'. George sighed. 'I'd like to be a professional footballer or some thing, but I'm not good enough for that. Just some thing for the next few years, say until I'm about 25 or so, and then look for a settled existence'.

Mike said that he was joining the Police in London, it is a good job, future, take promotion, it's got sports opportunities, everything you want, 'Why not try that' 'Yeah Mike' but what about the rest of the World. I have never been abroad, not even to Spain or France for a holiday. I am faced with another couple of years, on courses and projects'. There has to be something better than that'.

In London, the following day, the teams disbursed. They went their separate ways, back to their various homes. George and Mike promised to keep in touch, but both knew that the pledge wouldn't be kept. Each would go their diverse courses in life. George got the underground to Barnet, where he would catch a bus to Potters Bar, where he, his mother and father lived.

George's father was by education a chemist, an organic chemist. He signed on after the War, and had risen to managerial levels in the Brewery. Although George's father and mother were Londoners, the war years, had taken them to the Midlands, in order to research ideas and projects for the War effort.

Rugby then was the base for B.T.H. and English Electric, amongst other Firms. This perhaps protected it from being first strike targets from the Luftwaffe. In relative insignificance, not being a major city helped. This was where Jane, number one child, a daughter, was born in the Shipmans, and Paul, first son, and then later George. Mr. Shipman had worked for B.T.H. during the war.

The next eleven years had the three children settled in at Rugby, but them came the first upheaval and as Breweries were want to do. A take-over was imminent. They had to move. Jane was finishing her a level, Paul midway through secondary School, George was to start secondary school, In Leicestershire. Jane did go to University and later followed a life in Academia. Paul did his apprenticeship and went into Engineering and Technical Drawing. George was struggling for a future. A further move, from Leicester back to London, through industrial necessity put paid to any further academic studies, for him

What to do? Where to go? How to do it? The questions bounced back and forth in George's head all the time. I want to travel, see a bit of the world. How? What? Where?

"GEORGE' His father shouted. 'Here Pop, What's up? 'George, there are two parties of visitors coming on Tuesday for a tour of the brewery. Do you want to help with the showing around? One party is a group of landlords from Nottingham, the other, a bus load of guys who work on Oil-Rigs, from Lincolnshire.

'Yes, sounds good. I'll help out. What time on Tuesday?

'Come in with me to work and we'll go through the itinerary, and work something out'.

'That following Tuesday, was going to be a bit of a watershed in George's life, but he wasn't to know it at that time, but the next couple of years of his life were about to be taken up and well filled.

At 10.15 a.m. that Tuesday morning two coaches pulled into the Brewery yard. The first contained twelve couple of landlords most of the men had filled waistbands and red noses. The ladies, largish, chatting with each other, cackling humorously.

Tim Ryburn the P.R. at the Brewery took these over. He was a very enthusiastic and knowledgeable man in his thirties. He gathered them up, introduced himself and led them away for their tour of the plant. Kay Wilson was Tim's back-up. She was a short buxom woman with blond hair. She spent some of her evenings singing Country and Western songs at various hostelries. The workers called her their own Dolly Parton. She rounded up the Rig workers and George tagged along with them. The guys were different, fit, strong, no two the same. Some tall, other not so, but all with hard worked hands. The humour was earthy, in-house chiding and little anecdotes about themselves. Tales of other who worked on the Rigs. Disdain for softees and pen-pushers, hearty laughter at times, wry grins at other, knowing smiles and grimaces.

The tour was pretty basic for George. He was getting on really well with a large Dutch chap, who was a Rig Electrician know as B.J. was about six feet four inches, not so broad, but thin on top, with huge hands. How on earth he could handle small bits of wire was beyond George, but he was too diplomatic to ask. Getting inevitably came round to working on Oil-Rigs, and George was all ears.

B.J. promised to ask the Rig Manger if he could get George started as a Roustabout on one the many Off-Shore Rigs that the Company was operating out of Aberdeen.

All the chaps in that group worked for the same company, on different Rigs, but as they lived all quite close to each other around Grantham they had organized this trip. They Worked two weeks on the Rig, off-shore, then two weeks back. Some time is lost on travelling, but they preferred to live in England as opposed to near south from Aberdeen. Grantham was on the main train line north-south from Aberdeen to King Cross, for the overnight journeys to and from.

The tour over, and the hospitality beers being consumed, the Oil Riggers having virtually adopted George, and with the best intentions in the world, were going to get him started with them, offshore.

A call came from B-j about four weeks later. He had gone up to Aberdeen for his next 'Hitch', spoken to the Manager, done his 'Hitch' and was back. If George is still interest, get a ticket and go up with B.J. on his next trip, it was straight forward. Bring some work-clothes, better be warm ones, you don't know where you may finish up. You're on.

He met B.J. at Grantham, for their journey north. They had sleeper reservation, but not in the same compartment. A coffee at the 'Traveller's Fare was its usual crap despite the adverts in the buffet depicting fresh soups, cakes and sandwiches, there was only the foul coffee. B.J. said that that was all was there would be until wake-up before Aberdeen when the guard brought them a tea and biscuit. Hey ho! Let's get on with it. The train arrived, on they got, said their parting shots, and went to their compartments. A new day was coming, as at 6.00 they would be in Bonny Scotland and the grey granite town of Aberdeen.

The Oil-Rig that George was assigned to was a "135' Series. Thus named because the main deck was 135 ft. above the keel, which was not a keel, per se but the base of three massive legs that supported a triangular main platform. The legs were 30ft in diameter and 30 ft. deep. The legs were joined just above the footings by 9ft wide steel tubular sections. The entire structure was further strengthened by steel tubes, from the nice footers to the deck.

The Main deck, at the apex of the triangle, had the living accommodation, on two levels. The upper floor having the Galley, Offices, sick-bay, recreation room, quarters for senior crew and their ablutions, the roof being the Helideck. Downstairs were main crew rooms and ablutions. Level entry to the working areas. In front of the accommodations were the pipe storage areas, containers, and a crane on each side. The upper level was a catwalk some ten feet wide, from the accommodation to the drill floor, the epicenter of the Rig.

On the port side of the Drill floor, were the main engine rooms and mechanics stations. On the starboard side, storage areas and drilling mud pits and pumps.

Underneath the main deck were the office of the Barge Engineer, who managed the vessel. Beneath the Drill floor was the Moon Pool and Blow Out Preventer area, when not on the sea bed.

One set overall, one pair work boots with steel toe caps, one slicker suit, one helmet (hard hat) three pairs work gloves (useless when wet, but saviors of hands), 'Get on with it'. The Store man had a pretty 'cushy' number on the Rig. Thousands of parts to keep tracks of issue and returns. Manifests for the cargo coming on and going off the Rig, but he didn't get dirty very often. The Medic-Radio Operator wasn't too bad a job, but you did have to know what you were doing. When there was an accident, it involved serious bits of metal or steel, under pressure or falling. Theirs was an Ex Para Medic he was pretty good.

The lowliest job on an Oil Rig, where just about every non-specialist starts, is the Roustabout. Crews are deck hands (roustabout supervised by a crane operator) usually 6 and 1, drill crew (Roustabout, Derrick-man Assistant Driller and Driller),

3, 1, 1 and 1. The Driller was supervised by the night Tool-pushes or the Rig Super, who was the day Tool-pusher. Crews work a half day (just 12 hours) from midnight to mid-day or visa versa. The daily toil is scrubbing desks, chipping and painting, taking flow valves out when necessary and putting new ones in. On a wet day, one might be down in the pump rooms at the top of a leg. The job being to 'pull' a pump up, take it to the motor room for repair, then put another down to replace it.

George took to the life pretty well, and soon he was asking the Driller for some experience on the drill floor. He got his chances now and then. He wanted to keep learning the next job up, so whenever a vacancy arose, he could fit right in. He also went down to watch-standers' office, after his shift, to learn that job too.

When the 'Hitch' was over, a helicopter journey took the crew back to Aberdeen, and then there was the overnight train home. The two weeks off game him time to pass his driving test, buy second hand car, and get driving experience, taking trips to Cotswolds an area he really admired and enjoyed visiting.

There was a certain 'pecking' order, which he noticed after a few 'Hitches' On top were the Texans, or other Americans. Then came the Canadians. A bit below them, were the 'Newfies', the workers from the Newfoundland. After that were the Brits. The Newfies that George came across, were hard working, but so socially ignorant and aggressive. One day after the helicopter had discharged its cargo of new divers to the Rig, one of the Newfie drillers came into the dinning hall. He saw a coloured man sitting with the diver and said 'Who does that belong to'. The divers all took exception, but a stand-off was maintained. It was so unnecessary, but it showed the attitude of the driller.

When shifts change at midnight, one never really knows who to expect. On one occasion the day driller had just about worn out the 'bit' they had been drilling with and was about to haul out the drill string, when the shift changed. George was on the drill floor the night, and it was what hard work is all about. The drill string was about 9,000 ft. in total. It meant that is all had to come to the 'floor', change the 'bit' and then all go back down to resume drilling.

Drill pipe comes in roughly 30ft lengths, three of these together are called a 'stand' and so as each 'stand' comes out of the drill floor, the top end is at the 'monkey board' in the derrick. The rough-necks pull the bottom of the stand over to a section of the floor, out of the way. The derrick-man pulls the top out of the way, into the fingers 90 ft. above them. The process is repeated until all is out. There are at the bottom end, two or three stand of special drill collars, which are much heavier and more rigid before the drill bit. All of this sounds pretty straight forwards, until with a bit of maths one sees that it is about 100 stands of pipe, and it all has to be done as quickly as possible, to resume drilling.

To get the pipes stands disconnected the roughnecks use double jawed clamps, which are steel, heavy but counter weighted. Throwing them on to the pipe and locking them is physical effort, although to fit young men, who have the 'knack; it is not so bad. This is to break the tight grip between joints. The real pull is supplies by machine. However, this had to be done 100 times, and between that, pulling a stand of drill pipe which weighs nearly a ton into position. As the stand is pulled out by the drill works, 'slips' lock the nest stand in the drill floor (rotary) with enough showing to engage for the next lift. The stand is still in the drill works as it reaches the derrick man, who waits for the rough-necks to ground the bottom of the pipe, then he grabs the top and pulls it into a holding position at the top.

If it takes only a few minutes to do each one, then it is going to take nearly six hours to do it all. Then the 'bit' has to be changed, and it all 'run' back in, to resume drilling, that is 12 hours of solid hard work. A relief for each man comes from the roustabout so that a meal can be taken half way through.

Under normal drilling operations, breaks are allowed at three hourly intervals.' These breaks were called 'smokies'. The Rig cooks would prepare an urn of tea, and something to eat. Smoking was not allowed during some operation on the drill floor, but never the less, smokies were a part of the schedule. One day, the driller had been relieved by the Rig Superintendent, a large Texans we called 'Papa Bear'. He took a piece of the galley made cake, and took a great bite from it. After a few chews, he said, 'Just like Momma used to make, but she never used to shit in hers'.

Such dark wit was commonplace. During drilling, each time 30 ft. had been drilled and it was time to put in another section of drill pipe, a section was prepared hoisted up and made ready. If the drilling mud spurted out at the time of connection, it had to be cleaned up after wards. These 'wet' connections could be tedious, as when it was cleaned up, another connection undid all the work. One Canadian driller observed

'It's like wiping your arse on a wagon wheel, there just ain't no end to it'.

There was a good camaraderie in the crews. Hard shifts, a really hostile climate, cold, wet, and aching muscles, meant it had to be so. The two weeks sometimes flew by.

Working on Oil Rigs, can be dangerous. A length of wire line under stress, could snap. Then the wire could whip around, and, like a half inch wide knife blade sever an arm or a head, quite easily. If the Crane Operator, caught a container weighing a ton or more, and tipped it over it could do serious damage. Unloading a supply boat with a bit of swell in the sea, could be tricky. Pressurised container or valves had to be very carefully maintained to prevent mishaps. There was a lot to learn, and be wary of.

The supply boats when unloading, tied up to the Rig with a mooting system. This consisted of three inch chain links, from the deck level down to an aircraft tyre. The tyre was chained to another. A three rope line, was passed to the boat by crane, the rope line fastened to the tyres. Thus there was flexibility for the boat to ride the swells while ties to the Rig.

On one occasion, the tyre snapped. The boat untied, and the rope passed back to Rig. But repairs had to be done, in a metal work basket about six feet square and three feet deep, George and a colleague, were lowered by crane, over the side. They took with them some tools and a fresh tyre. Working at sea level they had to unshackle the chain, put in the tyre and re-shackle it up.

It was difficult working in such cumbersome conditions. The chain was rusting, so too the shackles. The tyre was large and awkward. Although they had waterproof on, the swell kept rising and flooding the work basket with freezing north sea. When they had it done, they were brought back up and allowed to have a hot shower, and fish work early. The supply boat captain sent a captain of cigarettes for them, on one of the 'lifts'.

George had spent about two years on the Rigs when his father came up with an outstanding idea. Mr Shipman had been to a conference where he had met brewers from all over England and some visitors from Rhodesia, 'George, if you want to see some of the world, get some real life experience and do some good for your future. Go to Rhodesia, and be a Policeman there for a few years'. He went on to say that he had met with a chap called Clive Townsend who lived in Salisbury, and is sending me the address to apply for the job. What do you think?'

Africa, the Dark Continent, Wild Animals only seen on T.V., Adventure, travel, George's imagination ran riot. It didn't take long to make up his mind to go.

The writing began, and application forms filled in. Once accepted, the Game was on. The deal was, that if one went there for three years, the tickers would be paid for. A contract signed, to serve for those three in what was known as the old, British South Africa Police

However, the deal with his father was this. He would be financially backed, should he need it, but, he had to complete the three years. Under no circumstances would his father 'bail' him out, if he were to fail, or shirk away from the contract.

The B.S.A Police was a descendant of the old pioneers' days under Rhodes. After a few battle with the African, his Company had taken the Country over. They had built road, towns, railways, and airfields. They had set up a British style Judiciary system.

Arrangement for the journey were made. A flight to Lisbon from London, then T.A.P. (the Portuguese Airline) from Lisbon, overnight to Salisbury. Photos were sent, details sorted out. George was off on an adventure of a life-time. He was to take with him, some early Christmas presents for the Townsends and would make their Acquaintance in due course.

Landing at Salisbury George Looked around for some sort of meeting party. A Police Patrol Officer (P.O.) should be there. He saw a chap in what looked like a Police uniform, and asked him if he was meeting him.

'You don't look like your photo much', said the P.O.

'If you look like your passport photo' George replied, 'You'd not be well enough to travel'.

'O.K. let's get you to your accommodation.' We've put you in a small hotel near Morris Course starts. I'll take of nights. Until the 5th when the Course starts. I'll take you there, and show you a few sights along the way'.

A whistle stop tour of Salisbury ensued and a quick drop off at a hotel and the P.O: was off, leaving George to collect himself, and get a rest, after the overnighter. The Hotel didn't have a bar, so he would have to find one nearby, for a couple of drinks later.

That evening, he had a bite to eat at the Hotel. He asked where a bar could be found. After listening to directions, he wandered out of the Hotel. In the tropics, sunrise and sunset are a very much set at about 6.00 to 6.30 a.m. and 6.00 to 6.30 p.m. so it was dark when he left. The overhead Jacaranda trees formed a canopy over the side of the road, which had a central tar section, with hard dirt sides for parking. This was disconcerting to George. He was now in darkest Africa, these trees may house poisonous snakes, which could drop on him at any time. There may the other 'nasties', lurking in the trees and bushes along the way too. There was no-one else in sight to take re-assurance from.

The only place that looked safe, was the middle of the street, which wasn't covered in foliage. With eyes and ears alert for anything and everything George made his tenuous way along the directions he'd been given. Some time later, after a couple of beers, the journey back wasn't so bad.

The following few days, were spent wandering around Salisbury, He opened a Bank Account. He found that he was getting very tired without a lot of exercise. Central Rhodesia is on a plateau, five thousand feet above sea level, The rarer air was why he was getting tired. He had to acclimatize. Maybe the Physical Training in Morris Depot would sort him out.

He walked up to Morris deport. It had enormous grounds and acreage. Apart from Morris Deport where he would be in Recruits Training, there were many other facilities. Of the building itself, it was of old grey brick, carrying some ivy up the walls. One part of the building was set aside for Senior Officers almost as a Private Gentlemen's Club. Trophy walls and Silvers Salvers.

Vast Fields were enclosed for the horse training and other equitational activities.

Shooting Galleries, with 'butts' and distances picked out. Targets called 'figure 11's which depict a shouting, helmet clad infantryman charging forwards, had to be shot at.

Newer building looked like classroom, lecture theatres, and other academic accoutrements.

George was rather impressed with his new opportunity. He had stated on his answer to his earlier questions. Who, What and Where. He had the where bit. What he was going to do, and who with, were as yet unanswerable.

A RUDE
AWAKENING.

Morris Depot was the only Training School for Whites in the Country, so all George's intake had come from hither and yon. He was not the only one who had to make friends from scratch. Some had known each other from various Boarding or Secondary school before, but it was a mixed bag all round. It meant life in a Barracks, with set times for set functions. Sleeping in dormitories of 8-10. Everyone got up together, breakfasted together. They dressed appropriately for the next series of lectures, equitation, etc en masse.

With his exception, they were all 18 years old, not old enough to legally drink, at that time, but there was a 'Mess' where they could. Most 18 years-old in the Country had had a beer or three by then anyway. One could serve the Country, but not drink in it.

The Training System as it was, still had an emphasis on horses, going back to when Officers patrolled the Country on hoof and boot. The Hierarchy must have been denied access to the Cavalry Club, but decided that the Regime must continue for the sake of continuing it. The pursuance of course, of discipline, and what they deemed Character Building. In any of the Station he clothes variety. It was customary, at every station, to have 'stables' first thing in the morning. This meant that at the beginning of each day, they would water the land-rovers, check the oil, and top up the fuel.

There were thirty in that Intake. The accommodation block consisted of three dormitories, mess hall, ablutions and a general purpose hall, for any activities that may have to be taken there when it rained. It didn't rain often, but when it did, it could bucket down. Having done Outward Bound courses and offshore work, he was sufficiently acclimatized to this sort of life. George was selected to do a shortened course because of his maturity, He would be excused Equitation. However, not before he had called Phillips. Instructor Phillips had a horsy face. It was said that he could eat an apple through a tennis racquet.

So, George was moved on to the Musketry section, under a much more pleasant chap called Mr. Humphries. He was a genial chap, rosy cheeks, balding a bit, about

50, he had done his policing in Palestine and other places, before coming here. He had found a niche here, at Morris Depot that suited him just fine. Teaching the youngsters the basics of the selected weapons of the Force, and getting them to shoot. The armoury had hundreds of the old 303's virtually W.W.2 stuff, which was being changed out for the Belgian 7.62 Self loading Rifles (S.L.R.s).

For the duration of 'Musketry', the sort of disciplines that all Military Units employ, were the same blindfolded, handling and 'proving', sighting etc. Similarly, with the P1, 9mm handguns, and shot-guns. Though he was never to become any sort of marksman, George picked it all up and quite enjoyed it

Square-bashing was done all together, as a squad. As usual there was always one who couldn't get the grasp of it. Officer O 'Shaunessy had a problem with left and right, and this led to him being picked out with such phrases from the Drill Sergeant as, 'O'Shaunessy YOU ARE LIKE SOME 'ORRIBLE CONTAGEOUS DISEASE. GET IT RIGHT! I know now why such men are often referred to as 'Drill Pigs' but they have a wonderful turn of phrase. One time, O'Shaunessy was invited to have pace-stick stuffed up his left nostril, or maybe some other orifice, due to his lack of drilling ability.

George was never to get too close with the others, they all knew that when they were discharged from here, they would be scattered over the whole country. Those who chose 'District' would go to 'Bush' stations, those who chose 'Town' could finish up in Salisbury or Bulawayo, or maybe some other large but distant settlement.

Too see the Country, George was to go for 'District' He would be a 'Bush Bobby'

Inspections cause the most hiatus, I would think that all those who have been in any kind of armed or disciplined civilian service have been through it. This fluffy of making sure you are looking perfect (or as perfect as nature allows) swatting of bits of fluff, which if allowed to remain would, rest assured, occasion such abuse from the Inspecting Sergeant as 'YOU ARE COVERED IN SHIT'. A little over the top maybe from such a small bit of fluff, but effect the time-honoured requirement of perfection in one's turn-out.

On one such inspection, a piece of cigarette paper was seen to be adhering to the chubby, fresh, 18-year-olf face of Officer Behenna. On being noticed by the Inspecting Sergeant; well he couldn't really miss it, inspired the exchange –

'WHAT'S THAT ON YOUR FACE BEHENNA?'

'it's a bit of cigarette paper Sir?'

'WHAT'S IT DOING THERE BEHENNA?'

'I cut myself shaving Sir?'

'HOW LONG HAVE YOU BEEN SHAVING BEHENNA?'

'Two years Sir',

'CUT YOURSELF BOTH TIMES?'

Physical Training is always a must at such establishment, George had been pretty fit in England, but now at an altitude of 5,000 ft, he found it really hard going at first. Breathing in, didn't seem to reap the same benefits as breathing at sea level. The mechanics of it all were there but nothing was going in, to help him recover after doing anything. Competing with acclimatized 18 year olds made him feel older still, as he grunted and puffed his ways around a track for what would have been a simple mile, subjected to the light hearted banter from the P.T.I. as 'PICK UP YOUR ASRE SHIPMAN'.

There were better things to come however. Class room work was fairly straight forward, there was quite a bit to learn, but it wasn't rocket science. Over the course of events, some of the lads dropped out. That sort of existence did not appeal to all, and some just could not adapt to barracks life. Reveille, up and at 'em early in the morning, being shouted at and verbally abuse. If one was not the brunt of the vocals then it was amusing, impressionable, immature youths, and fashion them to some coherent discipline body of 'fine young men'. The fact they were going out into the wide blue yonder as representatives of the Police Force, on leaving these hallowed grounds, a fair standard of training is to be expected.

Morris Depot was home to the Country's leading sports Ground. The Rhodesian Cricket Team, was host to a South African Provincial team in the Currie Cup. The recruits first operation was to make sure that the parking areas were Policed, parking orderly, and crowd control in general. Their leader was that day, one of the P.T.I.s, who was not really older than George, but was there by virtue of his representing the Nation, at throwing a hammer. Mr Mullins, who had the most immaculately polished 'Sam Brown' leather belts, a face that did not look just shaved, but really scraped free of any hint of stubble. He told them their duties and assignment and went to watch the cricket. This was going to be a good day perhaps.

On being relieved by a colleague, George made his way to pavilion for a soft drink. He took his drink to the rear of the pavilion where he could sit, watch the cricket and refresh. Mr Mullins was across the other side of the doorway from him, being pestered by a young lady, perhaps one of his groupies, for a soft drink. He was on-duty !!, and wasn't in the mood to be pestered, so Mullins said to the girl, 'Go and ask Shipman', she looked across, George ignored her (she was only a 14 year old) but she detached herself from him and as she came across, she said, 'Are you Shipman?'

Came the terse reply, 'If it's a soft drink you want, you'll be better with Mullins'. She left.

Watching the clock now for overstaying the break time there, he wanted to see a bit more of the cricket. The car-park was full, the game well under way, so little to do. The uniformed recruit wandered around the outer boundary, there is no stadium there, to worry about. The grounds consist of the pavilion, several temporary tents, for hospitality and refreshment. A white shin high fence outside the boundary ropes. Seating consisted of a small stand belonging to M.D. for more formal occasions like Passing-out parades, and deck chairs brought in for the day.

Straight in front of him, there were two block. Both had a beer to hand, and both looked as thought they had had a few beers to hand before those. One starts to buckle under, and tried to return the beer to his glass, but mixed with other things he had had, it fortunately just goes all over his trousers and the ground. Although dressed as an Officer of the Nations Police Force, George was not really one – yet. Hadn't done the course, got the 'T' shirt etc. However, he looked like one who had. He had to act like one.

As he approached, the buckled one, now on the floor, gamely tried to get up and pull car keys from his pocket. Being an Un-official- Official, George couldn't really let him get into a car, and try and drive, in his state. Not being really able to, or willing to, get into a situation of unlawful arrest or other mayhem, George, took his keys, and told them both that they were not getting them back, until he was happy that they were able to drive. This necessitate a few laps of the grounds and a few coffees to hand instead of beers.

Some 30 minutes later, a little chastened and very much in better shape, the pair applied for the keys, so the keys were returned and a hasty uniformed retreat was beaten, back to the car-park. The first Non-arrest of his career.

After a large part of the Course was complete, the sifting and sorting done, those that were there, were going to stay there. So it came to the turn of the Driving Instructors, to take the next stage.

George's experience with motor cycles had been extremely limited prior to this. He had seen a lot of them, had been pillion passenger on quite a few, unafraid, but was untrained or used to driving them. The Nations Police Driving Academy had a whole hotchpotch of them. Most were old, damaged, part-less, and heavy. The class was taken to a rough tack and hill site, and told to get on with it. The youth in this country, apparently, have trail bikes and the like from an early age, and handling these old Matchless' and Ariels was only a minor step up. Having fallen over with the brute a few times, and after having been accused of being an 'English Saboteur' for adding to the dents, he got the hang of it and managed to finish the lesson. He was later to go on a bike course, but that's another yarn. The car or rather Land-Rover driving, was a piece of cake, so the motor bike episode did not impede his finishing the Driving Course and alter being sent to a Station.

Life at Morris Depot wasn't so bad, as he had also learned how to drink the local beer. This is bottled beer which was seldom sampled in the U.K. 'Lion' lager or 'Castle' were the main brews, both of Southern Africa, and Mozambique (as it was) so when later he was to go travelling, there would be no shock to the system in changing ales.

There was the occasional time out of Depot, and on one weekend, a Bank Holiday, when the locals all went home, his new (old) friend, Clive Townsend invited him over to a stay at his place on the outskirts of Salisbury. He duly applied for the received permission (Clive was Police Reservist so deemed safe to be with), Clive came to the Deport, met him and off they jolly well went. Clive, Ann, his wife, a daughter, a slim, fun loving, dark haired, very eligible Penolope, and son Timothy had planned to spend the Saturday at Lake MacIlwaine, which is the nearest thing Salisbury had to a sea-side, some 20 kilometers from the City. They had small sailing boat which they towed behind the car, and a bar-be-que for lunch.

Timothy was really quite competent in a sailing boat so asked George if he wanted 'go'. Having never been in such a craft before, he said yes, let's do it. So Captain Timothy and his crew of one, took to the water and sailed across the lake, some mile and a bit, there and back. George had a whale of a time ducking under swinging beams and pulling bits of rope, up and down and leaning in and out of the little boat. The waves were at least three inches high, and the wind nice and steady a breeze as one could wish for. It was a really great day, so far from the norm, good company, and a new experience for him on the water. He enjoyed it thoroughly. Not the least getting to know Penelope (Penny) the bar-be-que, which here is called after the Africans a Braai Vleis, (burnt meat).

Sunday evening was back to barracks, he could not thank his host enough for the weekends. He was in for a lot of new experiences in the next few years.

One thing that was dawning on him while he was here, was the White (European) attitude in the Country.

There were so many facets and timbres to living alongside the African population. The Police Force, just like so many Colonial Forces, (Hong-Kong, Bermuda etc) had a senior officer level, and an N.C.O: type level, formed from African volunteers to the Police, (trained elsewhere in Salisbury) and this was a new scenario. The highest African rank achievable was that of a Station Sergeant, rising to there from Constable, a Patrol Officer, the lowest European rank, but Senior to the Sergeant. Many years. Another item on his agenda, was having a 'bat-man' which all European Officers had. An African servant to be employed, warranted some serious advice on this, but not yet.

By and by, the end of the Training Course arrived, and with little fanfare, George was to learn that his fist posting, was to quite a significant town, not far from Salisbury, in what was the Mashonaland, which formed a wedge shape from Salisbury to the border with Mozambique and a few roads connecting the main towns, with two arterial roads connecting Salisbury with Mozambique East Coast and the other North to Tete this posting was to Marandellas.

MARANDELLAS.

The headquarters of Mashonaland East District was a suburban satellite town to Salisbury. A wide tar topped road that went on to Umtali on the Eastern Border of the Country had its first major port of call here.

A Sign six feet long and three feet wide directed people to the turn off for the Police District Headquarters. Transport had been provided, by the Morris Depot vehicle pool. The driver knew the route, anyway.

An imposing, humped front lawn accommodated an elegant FlagPole with the National and the Police flags flying. Accessing the front door was a tarred drive-in area with a small parking facility. Two Jacaranda trees added a touch more colour to the façade.

The Main Building was a single story, white faced; block building, with a tile roof. The double door entry, opened into the Main Charge office. The front desk manned by an African Sergeant or Constable. It could easily contain twenty people. Further inside, a corridor passed the offices of the Patrol Offices and Section Officers. Deeper into the building were the more Senior Officer offices and the C.I.D.

Stretching behind the main building, an Armoury, Classroom and store, behind the main block, was a Parade Ground and the workshops. The workshops were converted from stables to house the vehicles and mechanics shops.

There were areas of well maintained lawns, shrubbery and trees. The taller trees game much needed shade to a the main building.

After reporting in, he was sent to leave his baggage in the single men's quarters and report back later.

The bungalow that was the single men's quarters, was set in its own grounds. Like nearly all the building he had seen so far, it was white painted brick, with an ochre roof tile. It had three bedrooms, a bathroom, kitchen, and lounge. The lounge was well furnished, with easy chairs and a sofa. Each bedroom had a large single bed, and plenty of cupboard space for all the uniform and private clothes accumulated. The whole place seemed ready to turn in to a fairly luxurious home if necessary. It was shared by the two, now three, single Patrol Officers. What a pleasant change from the Morris Depot barracks. It was just across the road from the Charge Office.

George was to share with Sid Ballantyne, a 19-year-old, fresh faced, dark haired lad, six feet tall and into his second year there. The third P.O. was Casey Stuart, another 19 year old, blond, five feet eight inches tall, blue eyes and of a really cheerful disposition. Both were pretty 'laid-back' in attitude. It seems that the role of junior P.O.'s was really just supervision of what the African Police had to do. It was the A.P. that went out on most of the enquiries and brought back the reports.

The town of Marandellas had a large European population, but seldom was there any crime or trouble from them. The outer lying area where the Africans lived was where the problems lay.

Carey took George across the road to the Charge Office. He left George to meet the Senior Staff and promised to find him a 'batman'. George was no really sure about that. How did one find a 'batman'. Visual images of the cartoon character swam in front of him. He could also envisage a liveried 'Jeeves' type of butler, with a head of ageing white hair and dark skin.

Being such an important station, its head was Superintendent Dunkworth. He was in his 50's full bodied, thin haired, and had been in the Police since there were stables, horses, and only dirt roads. To

George, he was a bit old fashioned, stickler for the book, and could be a bit pretty for detail. However, he was taken in to the Supt's office, at the far end of the 'L' and stood at attention while being addressed and formally introduced. He received what was, he thought, the usual sermon for new faces, and was taken out, this being done by the Section Officer, Fred Sweet, a very tall six feet four inches man, with fair hair, and an odd smile, as his face looked crooked.

To be a Section Officer one has to pass the exams on the first leg of the upward ladder in promotion. Fred had about 4 years service, and was about the same age as George

Next up, he was to meet the Chief Inspector, Raymond Ware. He was in charge of the station and its area. A slightly built man, five feet seven inches. He sported a moustache just a bit wider than Hitlers', efficient, brusque. A man who had mastered the Shona language, which few Europeans had, he even taught it.

That brought the morning around to coffee time. The recreation room was host to that, and it brought all the European Officers in together, (except the Supt, who had his served in his office). The atmosphere was really cordial and friendly. George met with those on duty and smile and hand-shakes all round. It seems that a high percentage of the Europeans had all come from some part of the U.K. and were making new lives for themselves under the African sun. the younger ones were second or third generation born and bred 'Rhodies'. The older once, had probably done service for the Queen in Malaya or Palestine, and not wanted to return to England. Similar to some Ex-pats who went to Kenya.

One chap Bill Lemon, had come here just a short time before George. He was an Ex Gloucester Policeman, who wanted a change. He was married and lived in a bungalow not far await. He and George go on well, and chatted about cricket. Bill had been quite a good player before coming out to Africa. He was five feet eleven, medium build; dark haired, with a bit of a shadow on his jaw late in the day.

There was C.I.D. group stationed here, but George seldom saw them, and they didn't mix that much, as they had a huge area to cover. Most of the outer stations in this district didn't have their own C.I.D. So the few that were at Marandellas had a lot of travelling.

A lot of the small talk centred on the forthcoming rainy season. It is mostly dry and how for 8 months of the year. From November to March the rains came.

The rains can make or break the whole of the Country's agricultural system, not so much the European farms that had cattle or irrigation systems, but the outlying African farmland and crop farmers. In the

Tribal Trust land (T.T.L.), Africans get land allocated to them by their Tribal Chiefs.

In most T.T.L. they would get about 6-8 acres per family and they would subsist on what they grew and raised. A lot didn't understand the principles of growing an excess and selling it for a profit against the future. The District Commissioner's Officers, many of whom were well educated Africans were constantly patrolling the areas trying to teach farming principles. Crop rotation, and building contour ridges, to prevent the loss of topsoil when the rains came, were priorities.

If the rains didn't come, there could be a drought situation in the T.T.L.'s which meant great hardship for the African, especially if it was two or more years in succession. Fortunately at the time Rhodesia was exporting grain to neighbouring countries and had a surplus for emergencies, but it is still a topic of much concern there. It was always possible too, that the rains may fail in one area and not another in a country so vast, two thirds again the size the U.K.

Communications were a bit problematical, as the telephone system didn't cover much, outside the main towns, so radios were used. No cell phones in those days. Police District had allocated call signs, Marandellas being given 201, and the other stations in the district 202, 203 etc.

All the Land Rovers has VHF radios and the stations had S.S.B. sets for the obviously greater range. This enabled one station to call another or to H.Q. in Salisbury from an outer station. Each morning, a schedule for all stations to receive messages from Salisbury (in the north) and Bulawayo (in the south) took place. A P.O. was to be at the charge Office for those schedules at 7.00. George was given that task the following morning.

Nearby all the vehicles used were Land Rovers. For the most part they were the personnel carrier type. They were painted grey on the body with a white rood. The side windows had metal riot screens, which protected the windows in the 'bush' as well. The vehicles had the front triple seat, and in the rear, two inward facing bench seats which could accommodate six sitting, and lots more if it got crowded.

Renault fours with the peculiar front handle gear shift, were used as General Utility cars. Three Yamaha R 4 motor cycles were on station for running around use.

At some stations, the Land Rovers were the 'pick-up' type, with open back. They had the bench seat in the front, and inward facing seats behind, but no roof. These were painted green, and used more at outlying stations.

Back at the single men's bungalow that evening. Carey had found George a 'batman', who was the brother of his own and explained what they do, how much to pay them and a few other tips. George's batman was called 'Ticky' which came from old sixpence that was used before Rhodesian dollars. In fact a few Africans were called 'Sixpence' presumably what they were paid. In Rhodes' time that was quite a good income. 'Ticky' was to be paid 20 dollars a month out of one's own wages. At first to George it didn't seem much, but then it's purchasing power was quite good.

His duties were to look after his 'Boos'. It meant cleaning the uniforms and boots, belt and other leathers. He was to make the bed, clean the clothes, and generally be a mother substitute. This is what the young Rhodesians were used to. They were brought up with servants. It was normal, most families had them. I was also an essential part of the economy, employing staff.

P.O.'s fed off the Mess funds, which were contributed to from one's won wages. Food and communal expenses were accountable to the S.O: (utilities the Government paid for).

'Ticky' lived with his brother and family on the outskirts of town, having moved in from the T.T.L. in search of work. This is what he was looking for, so it was good for him. A dollar being 100 cents, could buy quite a bit. A packet of 30 cigarettes was only 25 cents; a bucket of African beer was 20 or 25 cents; and if he wanted to woo a lady by buying her a beer for her 'services', that was 25 cents also. So for 75 cents, he could have a fair old time on the weekend. His clothes were his own affair, but most of the 'batmen' seemed to have work clothes which resembled fairly battered Police shirts, short and ankle socks. Shoes were usually made from old car tyres fashioned into flip-flops. It seems they get good mileage out of radials, but for now the rainy season, cross- ply's

George took him on without further ado and set him to ask, un-packing and straightening out his uniforms. There were various uniforms or dress-code. For the office. Brown shoes- oxfords; issued, knee length socks; a khaki colour with blue turn- overs; khaki shorts; green shirt; leather gaiters, with boots – brown leather, jackets – khaki, ceremonial No-1's they even issued mosquito nets. Catching malaria was a chargeable offence, as it was preventable. If caught, and an officer became unwell, one denied the Gov't of your services. Camoquine tables were taken every week, that was an order. Numerous other items, ties for example, depending on where one was stationed and the time of year (hot or very hot).

Cooking was done by the 'batmen', who could do extra amounts, and feed themselves also. It was not Garrick Club fare, but usual meals in the evening like a chop, potatoes and vegetables. For breakfast a cereal if one wanted. Lunch was often a sandwich as it was too hot to eat a heavy meal, siestas were not on the timetable Police stations.

If not on duty on the weekend, maybe a braai vleis was taken and let the 'batmen' have time off. Time off for the P.O. was very generous, the Supt insisted that they have one weekend off a month, (whether they need it or not) great!

George was to find out later, that at smaller bush stations, the weekend was more myth than reality.

At 6.45 the following morning George was the only European at the Charge Office. Next to the radio was a typewriter and paper. All the message had to be typed down as received. His skills in the secretarial field were not very hot, but as the messages came over, each section twice. His fingers ran over the keys well enough to faithfully record the messages. He didn't need a bucket of water in case he set the paper on fire, but it went well.

It was at this time, he met two of the African Sergeants. Sgt Mushewa was five feet six inches. He was of medium build, obviously dark, with a pencil line moustache. His English was Impeccable. If one wasn't looking at him, his diction and accent were that of educated public school type, but not 'plummy'. He could speak three African languages, his own Shona; Sinabele and Manyika . He had been in the Police about 15 years, and was a treasure for the P.O.:s. His experience and linguistics managed to accomplish all that was needed in investigation allegations.

Sgt Makunike was tall, a six footer, heavily built clean shaven, head shaved too. He was a very genial guy with a ready smile, he like football, and soon, with his good English they were talking football. He could speak Shona and Sindabele also. The African main languages of Shona and Sinabele reflect the major tribes of Rhodesia. The northern areas being Mashona, and the south of the country being mostly Matabele. There were many other smaller tribes and languages, however.

The Sgts were both chiefly, the link between the African constables and European Officers. The Constables could speak English. That was mandatory for recruitment. Sgts took the inspections, discipline and daily duties of the A.P. They were pretty hard on constables so the senior ranks would not have to shout them out. George liked them both.

Then came 'stables' the watering or the vehicles, top up with petrol, chick the oil etc. and the working day began. If one did not have any outstanding enquiries a road patrol was organized. They did that today, to show George the town and its hinterland. Bill Lemon was detailed for that, so off they jolly well went.

Most of the immediate area was straight tar topped roads in organized block. Plots of land with one bungalow to each plot, with enough around it to have a garden or a small swimming pool or tennis court. The whole area was flat, with nothing but 'Bush' around, to permit expansion.

When Rhodes planned the new town of Bulawayo, he did so that a sixteen span ox cart, could do a 'U' turn, In modern terms, it meant, plenty of side parking.

There was small Hospital, for casualties and two small wards, one for Africans and one for Europeans. There was a large bakery called 'Proton', run by a family of Greeks. This provided a large work force for the local Africans and cheap fresh bread.

On the outskirts of the town were the shabbier homesteads for the African migrant labour. There was a beer-hall here which sold cheap African beer. This was not dispensed in bottles but plastic tubs, which held about 2.5 litres, or half a gallon, (4 pints). It was brewed in Salisbury under proper hygienic conditions, shipped out in drums, and tapped in to the tubs or buckets.

'Chibuku' as it was called was made from grain, boiled and cooled. Chibuku was quite thick, it was like light brown ox-tail soup. It was not gaseous. There was a small alcoholic content depending on the sugar content.

The beer-hall was the site of many of the disturbances, not so much from drunkenness but arguments and fights over sharing it. Africans that had enough to buy a bucket, would share it with their friend, who sat around in circles on benches. They pass the bucket round, each having a swallow as it went. Well if one chap was telling a story and was not to be interrupted, the bucket stopped. Those to his right had to wait for their slurp. As the evenings wore on, others had their 'round' but impatience crept in, buckers spilled, and then fights.

If, as the beer-hall was open to all, some man fancied one of the ladies, for a bucket of beer she may surrender her charms. They could exit into the nearby 'Bush-land' out of site but within easy reach. Some preferred the cash equivalent.

The main watering-hole for the Europeans was 'The Three Monkeys' which was back in the bungalow area. this was frequented by most of the European Police (E.P.) the C.I.D. lads (well, naturally!) other singles and tennis groups for some Apres Smash.

Along the main road, were business, car sales showrooms; hardware shops, a café or two, all well back from the tar so that off road parking was generous and shaded with Acais trees. Parking in the shade got pretty important if one was to be parked for long. The cars got like ovens, in the sunshine. There was also the Rhodesia Railways station. The railway ran alongside the road, all the way to Umtali and then on to Beira on the Mozambique coast. It was a major export link to the coast the Rhodesia did not have, and a big trade route both ways.

They stopped for a coffee at one of the cafes and Bill introduced George to those there. It was not a close community, people lived their own lives, but it was not without a few, who lived other peoples' lives as well as their own. However after a while, just about everyone was on 'nodding' terms with each other. Especially so for the ladies, who spent more time in the shops than the men folk. Getting out to have a coffee with friend was quite a social thing, without inviting them home.

As a single man George was on the lookout most of the time, but here would be dangerous ground. Have to have a word with Casey!

Back at the Charge Office, there was a flurry of excitement as Fred Sweet was on the radio. It seemed that Wedza had lost contact with its mobile unit, and as it was last known to be coming our way, could we raise a signal from it. Repeatedly Fred called. 206 mobile 206 mobile, receiving over, come in 206 mobile. After a pause he tried again, nothing. Then came a plaintive voice over the air. I've rolled the Land Rover over, over'. At least he was in better shape than the vehicle.

The following day, George had to go and see the Chief Inspector straight away. 'Shipman you are taking Sgt Makunike, in a Land Rover, to pick up three witch doctors at Goromonzi, then take them to Mount Darwin. Trouble with Bandits had worsened so they are to go and do a bit of Hearts and Minds with the locals. Off you go'. So off he went to find the Sgt. Who would be his navigator.

The journey to Goromonzi was uneventful, other than the awful smell of a Tannery, which was the Salisbury side of Marandellas. A mixture of faces, rotting flesh, and chemicals, was the nearest thing to describe it. It was foul. Sgt Makunike had a cousin who works there, so he told me that they get the hides from all over north of the country, both game and cattle. They make things like waistcoats, shoes, hand-bags, all kinds of things there.

A respectful address from an African Sgt to a European Office, they use the term 'Ishey', which means something like Tontro calling the Lone Ranger 'Kimosami'. What they called you behind your back could be up to the individual Officer, but they all had nicknames for the P.O:s before long. The Africans were great mimics, and picked up the idiosyncrasies of people very quickly.

George asked Makunike why they were taking witch doctors anywhere. For the life of him, George couldn't understand why this day and age they were important. So the Sgt told him a story.

'Ishey, three months ago, a body was found in the Mrewa area, that is adjacent to the Mount Darwin area. It is mostly T.T.L. with some European farming. The body was of a man who worked on a farm there. That body was taken to a hospital to find out what caused the death, as there were marks on him. The Doctor at the Hospital could not find anything wrong physically with the man. A constable from Mrewa was sent out to investigate the death. He discovered that the dead man had crossed a Tribal Chief, by having intercourse with the Chief's daughter, who was unmarried. The Chief went to a witch doctor and paid money to him to put a curse on the farm worker. The witch doctor told the man that on the day he spoiled the girl, one year later, he would die. One year later the man died, and his body was found at his kraal.

'The African people still believe in these things Ishey'.

The three witch doctors were a 'rum' lot. They were all about the same height, which was below average, five feet six inches. They were dressed in long full length gowns, like a black surplus. Each had trousers underneath the gowns, all dark in colour. A dirty shirt done up to the neck, covered their bodies. Their hair was black long in ringlets. None of them was young. They gave an appearance of being old Jamaican 'rappers' with strings of beads and bones around their necks. A waist bah completed the ensemble. Two of them had canes about 2 ft long. Useful for pointing at those they put spells on.

Having picked up the three witch doctors they made their way to Mount Darwin in the north east of the Country. The tar topped road got a bit narrower, so that if there was an oncoming car, each went to one side to have one wheel on the tar and the other on the dirt shoulder. This was so with strop roads too. Passing traffic have a tyre on the tar strip, the other on the dirt. At Mount Darwin the three 'guests' were led off, and George and the Sgt parted to get a coffee at respective allocated quarters. They met up later and made their way back no Marandellas taking football, George was learning fast about do's and don'ts out here.

George learned from Sgt Makunike that the station had a football team, all of course African Police (A.P. and that they had reached the final of a local cup competition. The Sgt was coach, trainer and man with the sponge, He did not rate their chances of winning, as they were up against the 'Proton' bakery 'All Starts'. When do you train, and where? Asked George. He was duly informed and on the next training session he went to watch. What he saw was a rag tag performance of 11 individuals who didn't really play as a team. So in he stepped, advising receive a pass. Generally playing as a team needed vast improvement. The A.P. thought it was marvelous that an E.P: was taking an interest.

Their fitness was fine, but team play, un-cohesive. The final was not for a while yet, so there was some time to improve.

Makunike also explained the African handshake. George had notice that they were very soft.

'A hand-shake is not really and African thing. A touch is enough. When you offer the right hand, the left must clasp the right wrist. This will show that there are no weapons in your hands, and that there is no threat'.

The Supt had had a great idea. As Bill and George were that bit older and more mature, he wanted them on the promotion ladder. Both were called for and Informed that their duties would be changed. Instead of doing a day shift, and rotating with the other P.O:s for the later shift and being on-call all night. They would rotate the later shift between them, so they could both study for the exam in the evenings at the Charge Office. They would start next week, and Bill would go first. This was such a good idea that Bill and George were verbally challenged, as they neither had any ideas of studying or being promoted. The badges of rank were such that, with less than three years service merited a second bar. A Section Officer had three bars. Then Inspector who had the usual two pips. George had only been in the Country for a few months, this was jumping the gun a bit. However, after the exams it would be back to normal so give it a go.

The first week George was on his own, in charge of the Charge Office, he was informed that there had been a shooting and that the victim was at the local Hospital being treated. He got Sgt Makunike and off they went to see what had happened.

At the hospital the African nurse took them to a cubicle where a young African male had a small caliber bullet wound on his lower right leg. It wasn't life threatening, and he was being bandaged up and a tetanus injection, which probably hurt more than the wound. The Sgt ascertained, that said young man had gone to the house of the Greek who ran the 'Proton' bakery and been fired on.

Obviously he was not up to any good for being there, and was most likely considered a trespasser at least, or maybe a thief. However, he had been there, and the son of the Bakery owner had over reacted. The Greek had picked up a pistol, fired it, hitting the African's lower leg, injuring him.

The Sgt assured George that the victim was known to him, he wasn't going anywhere and had local employment for the Council.

Off went George and the Sgt the house of the Greek. George went up to the door, by now it was quite late at night, not lights on. Knocked on the door and waited. Being rather impatient he rapped again a little louder, until stirrings were heard inside. The son answered the door, so George enquired about the incident and told the lad to hand over the gun the son did as he was told after a bit of bluster, and left the door to get the gun, which he then handed over. George had no reason to think he was going to abduct, or flee to South Africa, or do anything stupid, so he took the gun back the Charge Office.

He put the gun in the safe, and wrote it all up for the C.I.D. to handle the following day. Which was what happened Unhappily, George was pulled out of bed at 08.00 to brief Inspector Ian Jack and Detective Roger Hill of the C.I.D. They would take it from there, for George, case close. It wasn't really closed for the A.P: though. Sgt Makunike must have told the story with a little more embellishment. He made it sound as though they had disarmed a serious gunman, saved the African's life, and was regarded a bit of a Hero, as was 'Ishey' Shipman. Facing up to armed men in the middle of the night. George just smiled.

On regular day duties, George spent an hour or so with the A.P: football team, showing them how to 'sell dummies' control and pass the ball. All basic stuff, but after the 'heroism' and now taking an interest in their football, He thought sunrise was at the top of his legs. The team were getting better, but were they ready to beat 'Proton All Stars'. Time was running out, and the day of reckoning was only two weeks away.

George's weekend off was coming up, and he was like a dog with a fresh bone.

When Penny from Salisbury agreed to meet up with him for the Saturday evening. She had a car, and would come and pick him up. They would go for a dinner out, and then she would return to Salisbury. Not as perfect as he would have liked, but a darned sight better than a beer or six at the 'Three Monkeys' with other cops as company.

One can get tired of the same people day in and day out. A bit of friendly 'ragging' was tolerated. The notion that he would take her to the African beer-hall, or bring her to the 'Three Monkeys' was dismissed. So that they could all do a survey of her was un-gentlemanly. He did however have to ask where they could go.

Bill came to the rescue, 'It's cheap, cheerful, very and 1 take the missus now and then. Just passed the railway station, the other side of the track, is a Chinky restaurant. Go there'. 'Oh! that's great, thanks Bill, I'll try it '. So that's where George took Penny on their first date.

She arrived at the junction of the Main road and the one to the Charge Office, bang on time.

Penny was in her little blue Austin Mini, which was her pride and joy. Her willowy slim figure and brown hair opened George's eyes and made his heart thump. She was dressed in black slacks with a pink blouse. She didn't need much make-up, only a touch of lip stick. Her complexion was lightly tanned with living in the sun, and her blue eyes captivated him.

He got in the car, and gave her directions. She was a positive driver and it only took minutes to get to the restaurant. It went very well, they chatted and laughed and time flew. So much so, it had only seemed like a flash, and the evening had gone.

He discovered that she was a nurse at Bindura Hospital so her time-off schedules were a bit tight as well as his. There was no was point in inviting her to his place, so they stayed until it was time for her to go. They agreed, to do this again, or go out for a day next time, which was a great Idea, take a picnic and spend quality time together. George would call her with his time off schedule.

He walked back to his new home with a million thoughts in his head. Life was looking up, indeed.

On the Sunday, the Traffic Cops had been called to an accident on the main road east of Marandellas near

Macheke. It was a fatal one. A car driven by an African male, had crashed into a lorry. I was detailed to go to the Post Mortem on Monday. 'How are you with blood and guts, George? Casey asked. 'O. K: as long as they are not my own', was his response. The local Physician Dr Winters, was in charge of the hospital, Area Coroner and Police Surgeon, and numerous other titles. One had to double up in District, as there was usually nobody else qualified. George met him for the first time at the mortuary next to the hospital. They got on well, and talked about local topics, while the African assistant prepared the body.

Everything was meticulously clean. The slab, the stainless steel utensils, even a bucket for the brains, shone. The sound of the saw cutting the top of the victim's head off was a bit off putting. A clamp had been put on the deceased's head, and the assistant was cutting round it. All done he stood to one side as the Dr and George approached the body on the slab.

Dr Winters put a gloved hand into the skull cavity and slid the brains into the bucket.

'Ah' he said, 'there it is can you see it? He pointed to the top of the spinal column and broken base of the skull.

Oh right' George agreed 'Is that it then?, nothing else?'

'I have already examined the body for any external marks or features relating to the accident, and so I'll write up the report. If you send some-one round to pick it up my office about 5.00 this afternoon, it will be done.'

Those in the Charge Office were distinctly disappointed at seeing George return, fine, in good colour, unaffected by the Post Mortem, George thought they had been running bets on how he would be.

The next Saturday was the day of the football final, a few posters in the area had gone up to draw a crowd to the local pitch. The Bakery had a good pitch, with benches for spectators, and although it was their home ground, by virtue of its condition, it was to be used for the final. On the morning of the game, the constable who was to be the goalkeeper, sprained his ankle. Poor Sgt Makunike was beside himself with worry

'I will go in goal for you Sgt,' volunteered George. 'The match was Marandellas Police side, versus 'Proton bakery side No? I am stationed here, I should be eligible to play.

At the ground, while warming up was being performed, a big 'Indaba' (Discussion) was taking p between, the referee, Sgt M. and the representative the Bakery. The White man was definitely not on their agenda. George was the only one in attendance and stripped for action. In the end, it was decided that he could play in goal, and the play could start.

The game proved a spectacle that amazed the crowd. Marandellas Police side beat the 'Proton All Stars' by 4 goals to 1. George faded into the background, as Sgt Makunike accepted the trophy, with a smile more like a beam across his face from ear to ear. The Africans who supported the Police side, were jumping up and down and whooping with delight.

On the way back to the Charge Office, George suggested that the Sgt present the trophy, to the Superintendent the following morning. Which he did. The dour Supt. actually smiled, but not being a soccer fan, he was just nudged into being proud that his men had done something good. He wasn't too pleased with George though. Being of the very old school in Africa, the fraternisation with the Africans did not score George any points at all. It may have even lost him a few, as events were to tell.

During the weeks that followed, the rains came, not wash outs but it made the atmosphere different. Cooler in the evenings, stickier in the day. George was out on a patrol, which took him to the foul smelling Tannery. He had to go in and take a look around. It was run by an Indian chap, who had been there for years. He was very obliging and showed George around. In fact, he stood George still, on a piece of card, and drew round his shoeless feet. He promised to make a pair of shoes out of game skin for George, which in fact he did. A constable out on a patrol brought them to George a few days later. They were comfortable, soft, and a perfect fit. The laces game-skin too. He had them for years after.

Another weekend off per month was forthcoming, so George telephoned Penny to see about a day together. He would wear his new shoes, to show them off a bit. It was arranged that they would go out on the Sunday to 'Mermaid's Pool' which was just north of Salisbury. 'Mermaid' Pool' is a natural water fall over a sloping rock face, which one did either on ones backside, or a waiters tray (returnable). Sliding into the pool at a considerable pace on one's bum, splashing into the clear water at the bottom, was great fun. The pool was large enough for a lot of people to swim, frollick and play about. Hanging above, was a rope which revellers clung to, either to traverse the pool or fall in. There were refreshments there, and it was a popular spot for young Rhodies to meet up and spend a fun day.

Penny wasn't too keen to go down the slope on her bum, which was pretty neat. She was slim and there was no spare weight on it to endure the bumpy ride. She did try it once after watching George do it a few times. He did offer to rub it better, but the offer was declined.

After 5 hours there, it was time to call it a day. Once again' they had both enjoyed themselves thoroughly, and each others' company greatly. Love was not dangling in the nor did serious romance really encroach, but a genuine friendship, that was going to last a long time. They with their first chaste kiss.

The next time George was on duty last in the evening came a moment of near panic for him. trying to study, Sgt Mushewa informed him of an allegation of Rape. The African woman was in the front office right than and there. Rape was something he hadn't come across before, and he was on his own. He could call for a more senior Officer to help, but he had to get the ball rolling just to prove his own competence.

'Right then Sgt. Have we any African Police Women?' 'No Ishey'

'We need to get Dr Winter here to examine her. We need to get her to the hospital to treat injuries. We need to get witnesses. We need to get the accused. How many men have we on duty right now for all this?

'Ishey, might I just have a word with her myself first?'

'Yes sure, find out what you can about the whole matter

The Sgt went away to talk to the woman, while George rushed back to his office to make a list of all the things he could think of, that should and must be done.

When he had listed about 10 things, he then tried to prioritise them before he lifted the phone to get some European help.

'Ishey. I think I have solved the case'.

'You have'.

'Well it is like this. The woman was at the beer-hall and she was propositioned by a young man, who offered her a bucket of Chibuku for her pleasures. She went into the bushes with him, and he had his way with her. On return to the beer-hall, he failed to buy her the beer and said he had no money to buy any. I know who this man is, but I think it is not really a case of rape. She did go to bushes of her own accord. She did let the man have his way with her, of her own accord'.

'If I give her 25 cents to buy herself a bucket of Chibuku, will that keep her happy and the allegation scrubbed?'

'I think that is a very generous offer Ishey, but you should not be allowed to do that, because then you will get these allegations every night. The Station would be full of rape victims. I will tell her to be on her way, and next time, get the bucket first, before going into the bushes'

'Right Sergeant, that seems to take care of that then. Yes, she had better be more careful next time heh!'

Exit one rape victim, to a very relieved Patrol Officer. Sgt Mushewa had really saved his bacon, preventing him making total ass of himself by pushing a panic button over a bucket of beer.

The Promotion Exams were due, and neither Bill not George were much the wiser for having tried to study, when they could. Along with other hopefuls from all over the District, they took their seats in the Conference room. Papers distributed, and clocks watched.

'Gentlemen, You may start', came from the adjudicator, Mr Ware. Papers were turned, and eager eyes started reading, George looked up and caught Bill looking at him. They were both lost.

An effort was made by both men, but some how, nothing seemed to blend the questions, to what they knew. It was forlorn task from the start. They glanced at each other again, stood and handed in their incomplete answer.

I didn't even undertand the questions, let alone answer them' said Bill.

'Me neither', mumbled George. 'I just couldn't fit them in to place, with what I had studied'.

They crossed the main road and headed for the coffee shop. That was end of any promotion dreams George would ever have in the B.S.A. Police.

Next week came the bad news. The Superintendent called him in to tell him that the rotation of Patrol Officers at Nyamapanda was up, and he was the next to go. It was a rotation of 6 months, with the customary weekend of per month, if circumstances allowed, or other duties didn't prevail. One P.O. was to return to the comfort of Marandellas, and George was to replace him.

That weekend a few beers were called for. It was, he told, customary for the P.O.s to give him a bit of a send-off. He had wanted to see Africa, now he was going to see it. Nyamapanda was on the Mozambique Border, at the end of the Rainbow.

Sgt Makunike presented George with a tanned Kudu Skin. It was A.P. way of showing their gratitude for the coaching and training that he had done with them,

The kudos that had all received from winning the local football trophy, had been a great fillip for them all. It was to stay with him for years.

NYAMAPANDA.

'**W**hy Me?, Why not You or Sid? I've only been in the Country for about 6 months and I am sent into the African version of Siberia.'

Casey was driving George and all his worldly goods and chattels (Impasha –Shona) to his new station. They had gone from Marandellas, eat to Mecheke, then north to Mrewa, then it would be north-east to Mtoko and the end of the tar road. Beyond Nyamapanda was Mozambique.

'Well, I play rugby for Mashonaland Police, so they want to keep me near Salisbury for the matches. Sid is a bit of a case really, He is so badly homesick, his folks live down near Bulawayo, they will be transferring him soon, when the next intake came out of Morris Deport. If he got transferred to where you are going, he'd go nuts. Besides, it is a darn sight hotter in Nyamers, than Siberia, look at the good side. We were on the Central

Rhodesia Plateau, same a Salisbury, on the 'highfield' now you are going out to the border, it is 'low field' you will be just above Zambezi escarpment. It will get pretty hot during the day you'd better take your camoquins, because the mosquitoes are much more fierce here'.

Mtoko was the last town where there was any European business or homes. After Mtoko it was all T.T.L. and without the District Commissioners (D.C.) consent. No European could have any dealings here at all, unless of course you worked for the Government, like P.O:s going into exile. The road was wide but the surface, unmade up. It was hard dirt, and after a while the resonance of the traffic's wheels made it corrugated so it became a real bone-shaker. If possible, if one went a bit faster the resonance would even out making the drive smoother. Scant regard for the suspension and shock absorbers of the vehicle.

It was 50 miles to Nyamapanda and there was nothing to see but trees and bush-land all around. Bush is not as thick as jungle. It is not open grassland. It is much drier, more open heat from direct sunshine, precious little few grain crops. They passed a few Native huts (Kraals) an occasional walker, an odd village store, which was made of brick without much mortar with a tin roof. These are also bus stops, as the bus that came by from Mtoko, was once a day which was regular but not often.

A few dirt road junctions led off into the bush, no sign post. If you were up here, you either knew where you were or you didn't. after 20 miles, they entered the Police jurisdiction of Nyamapanda, only 30 more to go. The station area was roughly 70 miles of border with Mozambique, and 30 miles in. This is sort of area is commonplace, in such a vast land. Some stations were bigger, depending on natural geography of boundaries such as rivers, gorges, some roads, and some political boundaries like T.T. L.s, town and city limits, and of course other Country.

The road we were on was the main road, seen on a map, as the arterial route from Salisbury to Tete and on to Blantyre in Malawi. A convoy of lorries comes through from Tete bringing trade goods from the north a couple of times a week. The convoy returns, taking goods out after reaching their bandits and thieves along the way. Any lone straggler could be prey, in these uncompromisingly hard and poor areas.

It was nearly lunch-time when they pulled into the Police camp. Ahead was the border gate, and small well kept shed for the Customs and Immigration post. The border itself was a barbed wire, four stranded, cattle fence. It disappeared into the bush to the south. To the north it went behind Police Camp, then vanished into 'bush'.

The Station was made of sturdy block, painted white, with a red corrugated steel roof. The stones that marked the walking areas were painted white. A few plants struggled to present themselves as garden in between. There was a 100ft tall radio mast, about 10ft square at the bottom and tapering up to a crows nest at the top.

Alighting from the Land-Rovers, they went in to report themselves as having arrived. They were met be a tall, late twenties, blond, harassed looking chap who was the Section Officer named Bud Johnson. They introduced all round, shook hands. Hel told them to take the truck to the single P.O.'s quarters, and unpack, Casey was them released to go back to Marandellas, first checking with Bud to take back some papers with him for the Supt. The P.O. who was to be replaced had gone on the morning bus, because he was due some leave before reporting to the Supt. It had all been sorted out by radio. George was to introduce after lunch. Bud turned and vanishes into an office. The station was bigger than the outside impression, it stretched back quite a way.

The Station considered of a small front enquiry deck and space. To the right was an office for the S.O. and a general office. Behind which was the domain of the past M.I.C.'s filing cabinet.

In the single quarters, George found an unoccupied bedroom and took it for himself. It was comfortable, nice bed wardrobe and dressing table. A window looked out over to a small pool and a small hut like building with a thatched roof. He couldn't make out what the sign outside was either. There was a bar-be-que near the pool, seats and grassy area. Walking into the dining room, it was all new-ish, comfortable, tables and dining chairs easy chairs and two large refrigerators. It seemed odd at the time but they were running on paraffin. He'd never seen a paraffin fired, chest sited 'fridge before. He opened them. One had food, the other was full of beer bottles, How civilised he thought.

'Hi, welcome to the arse-hole of the Empire. I'm Gordon Bradley'. 'George Shipman'. They shook hands. Gordon was of small build, five feet six inches, dark hair, light brown moustache. He'd been in the Police about 2 Fats, and had migrated to Rhodesia via Zambia. He was 23 and had a deal of good self confidence without being over sure of himself He explained that his back ground was from Africa. His father was a mining engineer and had been on the Copper belt in Zambia, before moving over to Rhodesia during the Independence of Zambia.

His father worked for Rio Tinto near Selous.

'Just arrived huh', Have you met the Boss yet?'

'No, I just bagged the room over there, and I've got to go up the Charge Office after we've had some lunch'.

'The Inspector is Guy Johnson, he's O.K. We all get along pretty well here, it's a small place so we have to. Bud is a bit of a worrier, but he's bucking for promotion and he's got a girl in Salisbury so he wants to do well, get promoted and find himself a move to town'.

'What's for lunch?'

'Sandwiches, usually tinned meat'.

'Do we live out of tins here?'

'No, it's just light and easy. We have a meal in the evening when it cools off. Go for a beer after work, then eat about 7.00'.

'Go for beer where?'

Gordon turned and pointed to the little shed near the pool. 'That is our own bar, The Gastric Ulcer, our emblem is the goat that you see in the 'Rhodesia Herald' 'Nubbin', the cartoon goat. Here come the sandwiches'

After lunch, George made his way to meet the Inspector, Guy Johnson. He was clean shaven, medium build, dark hair, and a pipe smoker. Aged about 40. George couldn't figure out why he was here, not married and with a posting nearer civilisation. The reason revealed itself later. Guy was divorced, cleaned out, and so he took 'bush' postings. With no white women within

50 miles and just his responsibilities to care about, he was fine.

Meeting over, and duties explained, George took his leave and wandered back to the Mess to unpack and have a look around. There was not just the police Camp here, but a semi-permanent Special Unit to do special patrols against the bandit problem. As Nyamapanda bordered with Mount Darwin at its furthest point there was always a chance of them coming down this way, to escape being chased from Mt Darwin.

Gordon offered the services of the previous P.O. 's 'batman', whose name was 'Tembo'. He was a young man, he had his first job at Nyamapanda, and was eager to continue. George said O.K. not really knowing how to judge anyway. Tembo was quite dark, had a caste in his left eye, but seemed to have done his work before suitably e was set on to make sure things were unpacked, bed made etc, while George had to write home.

Writing home was a duty, which could be a bit irksome. only person he wrote to was Mrs Shipman, his mother. She would disseminate all information, and would be upset, if upstage from another source. HC also had started to write to Penny. So both had to have the new address. A post office box number in Mtoko, was to be the destiny of his mail. The irksome part of informing his mother, was his own censorship. One couldn't tell stories which would make her fret, or have concerns that she supported the adventure, unwisely.

Thursday was day that mail was sent and received, as this was the day that the station had its day in court in Mtoko. It was a weekly run for Justice, mail, re-stock the beer supplies, and other essential purchases of food stuffs.

Bud ate with the P.O.'s Gordon and George, while Guy had his own quarters and arrangements. After dinner, all would usually congregate at the 'Gastric Ulcer' tell stories, swap histories, and down a couple of cool beers. These were ferried from the paraffin fridge in the mess, to the paraffin fridge in the pub. That evening, was one of great revelation, The Police 'Pioneers', who were so called because they built Police things in the 'Hell and Gone', were coming here. The existing generators for a bit of power, for the radios and a few lights, were not considered enough for today's modern requirements. New Generators with more power were needed. The Pioneers would arrive soon. Soon is a bit like the Spanish Mañana which means, don't hold your breath.

It was in the 'Gastric Ulcer' that night, George met two of the Special Unit team chat were stationed at Nyamers. 'Smokey' Bothwick was a Rhodesian, who had earned his nickname by letting of a smoke grenade during training The smoke had drifted to the President's lawn tea party, which was a few hundred yards away, who immediately decided that inside would be better. Medium height, solidly built and very fit, light brown hair cut short (regulation style).

The other. John Piper, who had hailed from Leeds, in a previous life. Tall; slim; small waspish moustache, the customary light Yorkshire accent. They had joined the Police, but preferred the more military style of enforcing Law and Order, they had a unit of African Police in camouflage, and their own 'dug-outs' within out camp, but their own section of it. There was another such unit, back down the road at Kotwas, but not present this night.

They all welcomed George, made him feel as though he had become part of a team, which was the camaraderie of Bush stations. Music was supplied by an old record player, when power was available, which was during the evenings. The acting bar-man for the evening, who was usually the same P.O: who 'ran' the Mess and its accounts, ran up the 'tabs' for those buying beers, and changed the records. There were cards, darts and 'lie-dice' for entertainment.

Lie-dice was a game in an old cigar box, where one stated how many dice were thrown, and what the outcome of the throw was. No player showed what was in the box. The next player was the one to his left, who accepted the declaration or challenged it. If accepted he would do the same, but he had to 'better' the throw, in the same sequence as poker hands. Thus, the first could pass a low pair, the next might make two pairs, and so on until towards the end Here the cheating started, and one dice was thrown, to convert a 'full-house' into a straight run. Accepted at one's peril, but it was only for a few beers, and a good deal of fun. Never were stakes to go above that level, and while George was at Nyamers, nastiness just didn't occur. If one didn't want to play. O.K. Don't.

Routine at Nyampanda was much the same as any other station. Stables, radio messages, supervision of the AP; road patrols. The African Sgts were again to be a great source of help to George. Sgt. Matambara was a hefty thick set African only about five feet six inches with a wide grin and thin moustache. He and I were told to go out to check on a kraal where a certain African lived. This chap, lived in Salisbury, whose home kraal was up here had been arrested. Salisbury wanted to verify his home address. Matambara drove the land-rover as it rattled and bumped its way along the main road, south to Mtoko. They saw, in the middle of the road, walking, a single African woman. She seemed to fail to hear or acknowledge the noisy vehicle, until they were right behind her, then she jumped with fright to the side.

'Ask her where she's going Sgt.

Matambara stopped beside her, and got out to speak to her. George noticed a piercing of her lower lip, with a 2 inch long piece of grass stuck in it. He said nothing., wondering if it was a Tribal thing. She had a flat, worn, lived-in face.

'Ishey, she is walking to the leper colony in Mtoko'.

'That's miles away, did she miss the bus?'

'She had no money for the bus, but she will walk all today, visit her husband there tomorrow, and she will walk back the next day'.

'Is the O.K. out here, can we help?'

'No, she will be alright, it is quite usual'.

The Sgt got back up into the rover and started up.

'Sgt, what's the piece of grass doing stuck in her lip, is it a Tribal marking?' 'No Ishey, it is for beautification'. 'Doesn't seem to work with her does it?' 'No Ishey', laughed the Sgt.

They turned off the main road and onto a narrower road, with grass growing in the middle of the wheel tracks. All round were low trees with thin trunks. After asking, George was told that these were called Mopani trees, and it was the trunks of these Mopanis that kraal huts were made from. That and muddy wattle made the walls, with a thatched roof, made from grass. Hence the local expression 'Pole and Dagga' hut.

The Sgt responding to George's questions was education him with a few Shona words and customs. He had wanted to see the World, and now, thousands of mile from England, he was doing just that.

They reached the kraal they required by the simple task of asking. From the Chief of the Tribe down, them are (depending on the side of the Tribe), elders, and kraal heads, who comprise the Council that sits with the chief to decide on matters important to their T.T.L. They allocate the portions of land to each family. So the Chief's kraal knows where they are all at. The normal size of allotment here was about 6 acres. The families became subsistent crop farmers, and had to do as they were told by the Chief and his representatives. The Chief held courts to decide issues such as Libolo.

When a man wants to marry a woman, he must arrange with the father of the woman, a bride price. He must pay that price before the marriage but could negotiate should the price be high. If, for example, the woman was educated or skilled, the price may be as much as hundreds of Dollars. It could be several head of cattle, pigs or chickens. Failing to pay his instalments, the father could take him before the Chief for punishment of some kind. If she was a bad wife, and didn't work on the land very hard, or couldn't / didn't have lots of children, the man could take her before Chief's court and demand a divorce. Should his case be proven, he was entitled to claim his Libolo back.

A divorced woman's libolo price, as second hand goods, was low, and a bit of a disgrace, within the Tribe. George had mental visions of the British equivalent of 'Grab a Granny' at the Dance Halls throughout England. You may find yourself a wife, and only have to pay her father a crate of light ale for her, if she was no virgin. This does however make it a serious matter, if one despoils a maiden, the bride price is diminished and the father loses out considerably on that deal.

'The kraal found, luckily quite near to the road, only about a hundred yards off it. The two parked up and walked to the kraal. A working woman with an infant on her back (obviously a good wife) was the subject's mother and verified their enquiries. There seemed to be more woman than men here. The Sgt told George that another custom of this area was, that if a man's brother died, he took the responsibility of his brother's family. He adopted the wife and children into his kraal, so they could never be without a home over their heads. How far this stretched, as regards brother going to Salisbury, he didn't ask. Trying to equate that to U.K. behavior patterns ran his mind ragged. Imagine having to house your brothers' wife and family if he went away or died. On the one hand it could legitimize sharing a bed with one's sister in law, which could work many ways. Then of course, there would be one's own wife to placate on that issue.

An African could have many wives. If he can afford libolo and pay for them. The tricky bit, would be keep them all happy. The African women were very much subject to the will of the men, then. The first wife may be the most important, but the sexual side of things, must have been very awkward. This was not a religious thing, it was a tribal custom.

Back at the Station, radio messages sent to Salisbury, the enquiry completed it was the end of the working day. Travelling around on dirt roads takes much longer than the smooth passage of tar, and covering an area of 20,000 square miles would take for ever. The area had, of course, been divided up into Patrol Areas, these were 4 days stop-outs. That was to come.

The two European Chaps from the Customs and Immigration post came up that evening. The Customs chap was small, reminded George of Toulouse Latrec. Small goatee beard, very slight stature, and short. The Immigration fellow was a big softee. He was an Ex-Brit, but despite being above medium height he was overweight, and a bit flabby. Nice enough guy however called Oliver Dale. Toulouse Latrec's name was Jani De Vries. They shared a Mess, behind their working

Border Post, which was another small Government bungalow.

The Convoy had gone through while George was out, and Oliver had his new supply of Piri-piri peanuts. These bagged nuts had a hot spicy coating, and could not be obtained locally, so he got one of the regular lorry drivers to bring some for him. Oliver wouldn't share his bag of nuts. 'No, get your own, get off. It was after 7.p.m. and getting dark, the beer had threaded its course through and demanded release. Oliver left the Gastric Ulcer and went round the back and was gone just a few minutes, and there was a cry of anguish. Oliver came running back, past the curious crowd, and up into our Mess. 'AAAAAGH, OOOOH, AAAAGH Jani went to investigate, and found Oliver with his penis in the sink under the running cold tap. Jani returned to the 'Ulcer', and told all, that the hot piri-piri from the nuts, had been transferred by his greedy fingers onto his Dick and started to burn. Of course, every body found this highly amusing so it was Ollie's round.

It wasn't to be Ollie's week. Two days later he found swellings on his buttocks and went to Mtoko hospital. There they found maggoty grubs under his skin. His batman had left the washing out on the ground, instead of hanging it up. Blowflies had laid their eggs, and he had worn the underpants prior to their being ironed. e eggs had buried themselves under his skin, and grew there. He did however receive as an apology, a goat, from said batman. He and Jani called it 'Nubbin' after the cartoon in the paper.

Government vehicles are specially trained to break down, and demand attention every so often, especially when hammered about on bush roads. Based in Mtoko was a mechanic, who covered a huge area, for the repairs of government trucks. 'Gasha' Tinsell was one such mechanic. An Aussie, five feet four inches, evenly built, clean shaven, and a really lovely fellow. A traveller on life's highway and every day he was happy to be there. If he had to come over to Nyamapnada, often as not, have supper with them, a few beers and they would find a bed for him for the night. No point in facing a 50-mile drive at night, especially after a beer. 'Gasha' told wonderful stories.

'One night' he related, 'I was in a posh Sydney nightclub. I was getting really drunk, when one of the 'heavies' came over to me. The bloke was a foot taller than me, and about the size of a second row Wallabee. I told him that if he didn't give me a drink, I would smash the place to bits. So he brought me a Coke '!

Christmas came with an air of an ordinary day. It was a clear hot, sunny day. It just happened to be December the 25th. On call that day was Guy. Bud was on his weekend leave in Salisbury Inspector Guy was doing what ever he did, but George had no permission to leave Camp. The special Unit P.O.'s were around, so a bar-be-que was organised. Dress order of the day, was swimming trunks and bottle openers. The bar-be-que was a three sided, two feet high brick arrangement with a fire underneath. The cooking was done inside an old plough-share. The meat cooked on the upper outside of the 'share. Gravy was made from onions, tomatoes and beer as it was poured over the steaks and down into the bottom of the plough-share.

They had managed to get some strange South African sausages called Boerewors, which cooked in with the steaks. A sort of salad was concocted, with tomatoes and whatever could be found, and a pot of 'Sadsa'. Sadsa is the staple diet of millions of Africans from the Sub-Sahara to Cape Town. It is a porridge made from Maize. (Sweet corn, corn on the cob, whatever). The corn is allowed to dry under the sun. The cob is stripped of its seeds, leaving the husk to be discarded. The seeds are then ground into powder, or rougher, into a gritty, like salt, form. A pot of water is heated to boiling. The grains are added until it forms a thick porridge consistency, thick enough to take in the hand and mould into a small ball. Every-one shares it, each taking a ball, dipping it into the gravy and eating it. In civilised parts, it is spooned onto the plate and eaten with a fork, like mashed potato. There are more hand feeders in the World, than knife and fork, or chopstick eaters.

The steaks had been provided by Special Unit, ad luckily strayed upon a suicidal Kudu. said bad run in front of target and sadly died, 'Big bag of Oranges' had been picked up, brought to camp, butchered and distributed among the Camp. The Africans loved the body and head meat, while the Europeans had the quarters. Nyamapanda, being 'bush' station had a hunting license, For the 'Pot', by the District Commissioner. With the extra mouth; to feed with the Special Units, an accurate check of the use of the license was never really kept. A smaller animal like an Impala was deemed to be a 'small bag of oranges' for radio purposes.

John Piper and George decided it would be a good idea to have a look around, so they climbed to the top of the 100ft radio tower, to a small crow's nest at the top. They could see for miles, across undulating greenery which were the tops of the Mopani trees. Far to the north was 'Baobab Beacon' the very tip of their territory, where the Mazoe River leaves Rhodesia into Mozambique. To the east lay more of Mozambique and the border down to the Inyanga mountains. To the south for roughly180 degrees was theirs. The southern edge of the station's area was the river Inyamsizi, across that was Inyanga

North station, There was a sort of road that went along the border, from Nyamers down to the river. It was just a very bad dirt road and seldom used.

The tribesmen that lived this side of the border had relatives on the other. To visit was no problem, just get over the cattle fence and see your cousins. any such visitors were caught, by the Customs and Immigration Africans, Ollie and Jani, would send them back. The only inconvenience, was having to keep to the dirt tracks. None of these had passports or anything, it would be totally futile exercise trying to enforce or guard a TO miles plus, cattle fence. Political boundaries had no in family or Tribal requirements. Tribes all around the borders of Rhodesia, had kin in the neighbouring Countries.

The Festive season was thus spent. The only crisis being, how low on stocks the beer was getting. 'Smokey' was off to Mtoko for supplies the following day, so reserves could be topped up, problem solved.

Rains were imminent, and a few days later, a storm blew in. It was refreshing in many ways. It cooled things down, and was good for the crops. It made a total disaster of the roads, which were awash in every gully, so the Camp waited it out. After the rains had eased a bit, an African came to the station with a report that a man was dying in a nearby kraal.

George was on call and went out in a land-rover with Sgt Chamutsa, an young newly promoted African, a Manyika by Tribe. Fresh faced, raring to prove himself. The informant got in behind them and George drove down to the border road. After the rains and being dark, it was a tricky drive. Some of the road was ruined and he took to the bush a couple of times to get around wash-outs.

The kraal was found, and sure enough, an African was lying on the ground with blood over his body. He told the Sgt to get the story, while he went to the first aid kit in the vehicle. The African had wound to the chest, which had gone into the lung. It had been caused by a knife, which was never found. The first aid kit did not have what George wanted, so he improvised. To seal the chest wound, he got some large green leaves. These he wrapped over the wound and bandaged them tightly around the torso of the victim. Now to get him to hospital.

Ripping a door from a hut, that made a stretcher. Recruiting from the crowd that had gathered, they rolled the patient onto the door. Four men to lift the body up and into the back of the land rover. Fortunately by now the rain had let up. Chamutsa had questioned the inhabitants of the group of huts, the assailant was back over the cattle fence and gone. Driving back up to the border crossing at Nyampanda, George went straight to the main road, and drove through the night to Mtoko. It was a dark night, with no moon, due to the cloud cover.

A nearly two hour drive, with Chamutsa keeping a eye on the patient, with a huge sigh of relief George reached the tar road and the hospital. Casualty took care of the victim, so what to do next. George decided to wait until morning for the drive back, so he asked the hospital staff where they could sleep for a couple of hours. George got the padded examination couch, three feet from the floor and just about as wide as his shoulders. The Sgt got the bench. Each got a blanket.

In the morning, they were roused by a nurse, bearing cups of coffee, which was a nice gesture. George was complemented on his first aid, which had saved the chap's life. The hospital had no refreshment facilities so after a radio message to Nyamapanda to report in, George had to pick up the mail and then make his way back.

Weekend leave was due for George, he had written to Penny and planned a weekend together at her parents' home in Salisbury. He got a lift in with the convoy, and a taxi to the house. That evening they went out for a meal, and discussed a trip for the following day, up to Kariba.

The road was a good, wide, double tar surface. Kariba was north-west, and roughly 350 miles from

Salisbury. The distance was not really a problem, because although it was a long way, there was little traffic on the road. They stopped upon the way at a wayside orange stand. Here in a three sided wooden shack, with a counter at the front, fresh orange juice was squeezed into plastic cups.

Standing there, enjoying the drink, they gazed at the splendid view. Fields covering hundreds of acres of orange groves. The full rich green of the leaves contrasted with the bright orange of the fruit. The trees were in impeccable military lines, hundreds of them.

Ahead of them was the Hunyani river valley, and beyond that, the Hunyani Hills. The town of Sinoia nestled at the base of the hills. They could just make it out through a minor heat haze over the river. They carried on, and arrived at Kariba, for a late lunch. They ate at a restaurant over looking the Dam. wonderful feature of 2011' Century engineering. It was not permissible to cross over the dam, as Zambia had their border. The dam did supply millions of watts of energy to both Countries.

The rains had not been so good, so the water table in the dam was only high enough to open one of the sluice gates. It was still, spectacular. There is something majestic in seeing the might of a dam holding back, the waters of a lake, created by itself.

The Africans believed that the spirit of the river God Myaminyami exists there. Before the dam was built, Kariba was a natural gorge. In full flow, the waters squeezing through the cliffs, caused such turbulence that the presence of a river God was inspired. Below Kariba there is still white water rapids. Many lives had been lost, before the dam was built. During its construction, many Italian prisoners War perished in the building of the Dam.

The Lake stretches about 350 miles towards Victoria Falls. There are National Parks and Game Reserves along its banks. The Animals are protected by virtue of access being denied, to anyone other than specific Government groups. Boaters on the lake can watch the 'Game' ng as they don't get too close or interfere in any Elephants, Hippo and crocodile are the easiest to spot' but antelope and lions are in the parks too. Fishing is J popular sport on Lake Kariba also. George and Penny got back late, having had a meal on the way back. A lie in Sunday morning was called for. penny had much to chat to her parents about as she was away from home too, in Bindura. A quiet day spent with a few drinks out, later that evening.

Up early Monday, to make his way back to Nyamapanda. He felt a new man after that brilliant break.

'The unused land at the rear of the 'Gastric Ulcer' could be cultivated for some vegetables and things' George put the proposition, to Guy. 'If you want to, that's fine' He replied.

So, taking Chamutsa to one side, George surveyed the ground and divided it into strips about ten yards long by one wide. There would be enough for the African Sgts and Constables to have a strip each, and grow some vegetables. On the understanding that George had a strip, and that a few of the veggies could be used by the Mess. George didn't want vegetables he wanted to grow some lettuces for the salads. Work went ahead, the strips marked and dug. Lettuce seeds were bought in Mtoko and irrigation done by the camp labourers. There were two of them, who kept walls up, appropriate stones painted white and various other duties. Everything fell nicely into place with the scheme.

Then, alarming news came from Jani and Ollie one day. The convoy, which had come down from Tete, informed them that a cholera epidemic was spreading south, towards the border. The facilities in Mozambique, to prevent or control the disease were nil. The little bit that was there, had a few medics, but nothing hold up an epidemic sweeping across T.T.L. like a Customs, Immigration and police sent radio messages HQs. The response was at first disbelieving. No word had reached our Lords and Masters from Official sources. So how could it be so. Wait until the epidemic reaches our T.T.L.s. THEN something might be done. It might never happen. Heads back in the sand.

Sure as sure, the epidemic came, a week later. Reports from the T.T.L to the north of the Camp told of dehydration through vomiting and diarrhoea, and death.

'What we have to do, is to isolate the T.T.L. until serious medical help arrives'.

Guy was addressing The E.P. and the Sgts. buses which travel along the sides of that T.T:L. have to stop. Roadblocks to be put up, to stop locals leaving the TTL'.

'I know it is farting against thunder, trying to stop movements of residents but once they know that should be isolated to prevent spreading the disease, may contain it'. Special Units were roped in to help Salisbury decided to send us some pills. No drips, ambulances, none of that. They still didn't happen. Or, they didn't know what to do themselves.'

Eventually a team came from the hospitals at and Marandellas. The containment had worked quite well or those that fled the plague had not taken it with them. It was George's turn for a weekend off, but he was told he must report to Camp Hospital in Morris Depot for more pills, or a jab. Once of the P.O.'s at Mtoko who had a pass waited for him and together drove to Salisbury.

'Do Not drink' after this injection. Said the Doctor. What the hell use is a weekend pass if one can't have a drink.

He wasn't seeing Penny as she was not on leave from Bindura. He could stay in the Special Unit Mess in John's place, but not allowed a beer. Come On!

George's will power lasted a few hours. He was amazed at what the bush had done to him. Wandering around a big city was a thing of amazement. Oh look a bank. We don't have banks at Nyamers. Oh look an office block. I haven't seen one of them for ages. In a supermarket he wanted to touch a white woman. He hadn't done that for what seemed eternity. The woman backed off a bit at seeing the look on his face. I better get out of here. All this was going through his mind. He had heard about people getting a bit bush crazy, he had the first signs of it.

A bar that P.O.'s use as their favourite watering hole while on leave, presented itself to him, during those later ours in the evening that the Whites called 'Sun-downer time. he met a couple of other guys, who, like himself, have a weekend off, need to get away from the District Station, but have not got much to do in Town. A few beers later, George wandered back to wash and change before going out that evening. He lay on the bed, blacked out, and didn't wake until the following morning.

The man had said 'Don't drink' He had, and lost 12 hours. It wasn't until he got back to Nyamers, that his loss proved so much

Regulations for controlling the epidemic had stated that all vegetables had to be boiled before consumption. He had the only lettuce patch in the area, and boiled lettuce would not be on the menu. They were doing so well too. Back to square one with the allotment. The epidemic petered out, with only twelve deaths, numerous saved by the medical teams. No acknowledgement of the epidemic officially.

George's first four-day patrol, was to the south of the Station. He was to take the border road down, then cut inland to Chief Chikwizo's kraal, then deal with a few Of the same type of enquiries he had done before. Radio in every morning and evening, where they camped. There were some old D.C.'s camps in the area that still had water. For lighting it was hurricane lamps, cooking on an open fire. He would go with Sgt Matambara, and take Tembo along because he was from that area.

Loaded up and set for action. Armed with a shotgun and a rifle, some food, radios, etc. off they went. Having to do a report at the end of it all, George took notes as he went. The state of the roads, after the rains, to be included. The state of the border fence for any future attention, kinds of things to be observed and written ups. The first day was un-eventful. He did learn that Tembo was soon to be married, so they talked about the libolo and where he was to live. Tembo was O.K: with the price for his wife, but it left him short of a hut.

'How much do you pay for a hut' asked George.

'Well, Ishey, to get someone to cut down enough Mopani poles, and gather the thatch, my brother will do that for nine dollars. The work of putting it up, my wife will do with her sisters'.

'O.K. then, I will give you the nine dollars as a wedding present'.

'Thank-you Ishey, I will tell my family tomorrow'.

So Tembo got his first house, as a wedding present from George.

'Chief Chikwizo's kraal, was a spread of about eleven huts. Chickens ran around, real free range. Some pigs snuffled at the huts where the sadsa was being prepared, and the husks available to be eaten. Two women were at a hollowed out small tree stump, with baseball bats, thumping down on the seeds, to grind the corn to grit. They worked as a team, one thump down, the other lift up. George thought they must have shoulders like Olympic swimmers to be doing that every day.

The Sgt brought the Chief up to date on who we were and why we were there. 'This is a courtesy that is observed going to a Chief Kraal. He may have been having a court session, or other Chiefly duties. He was to have a small court that day, and he knew of Tembo as a member of his tribe, and of course the libolo negotiations. He was very impressed with George because of the gesture to pay for the hut. George had brought with him some packet cigarettes as a gift for Chikwizo.

African bush cigarettes were dry crumpled up tobacco leaves, that grew there, wrapped in a bit of Rhodesia Herald newspaper, and were a acrid smoke, if ever there was one. Having proper cigarettes was a prestigious 'prop' for a Chief to be smoking. In return, Chikwizo gave them a chicken for their dinner that night. George was never sure who got the best of the deal there. The chicken was so tough, it was like 'Road-runner' It must have clocked up a thousand miles around the kraal before it was killed for food. However, it all went well, so the patrol continued.

They camped up char evening at an old D.C.'s camp, had the chicken and retired without fuss. The Imyamsizi River was only about 20 yards wide. It had got crocodiles in it, but none came for a photo shoot that day. The locals had stories of crocs taking goats, by the waters edge. There were no cattle in that whole area because of tsetse fly, except for a control herd of the D.C. A lot of Africans were disgruntled by the fact they could have no cows but the D.C. could. The zoology of the reasoning was lost on them.

One place that was a must to visit was 'Lawley's Concession'. In past years a D.C. had given a white man, Mr Lawley permission to have a business enterprise in a T.T.L.

There was a tunnel entrance, about 4ft square leading into a hill. The rails that came out carried a wooden trolley, on solid castors that held about a cubic yard of rocks. Three Africans were working there, one pushed the trolley to the top of a wooden chute. He spilled the rocks out, down the chute. At the bottom of the chute, three hammers, their shafts lifting and falling on the rocks, as the cams at the top rotated. It was driven by a wheezing old motor that gave off smoke as it laboured. The other two men were superintending the smashing of the rocks, and then in a brook below the chute, they panned for gold. It was like watching a re-run of an old Wild West movie, where some gnarled old-timer swilled the dust around a handle less bowl.

The two policemen went down. George was amazed at this. Actually panning for gold. After a few minutes, of watching the miners at work, one brought the pan to the Sgt and George and showed them a few flecks of gold. He told them that the mine harvested about 5 grams per week. Rhodesia at one time was a leading gold producer, but not much from this area.

They drove on to an African store and brought some ready ground sadsa, and some tins of stuff to go with it. Tembo had picked some leaves that he said were edible and could make some 'relish' to go with the sadsa. They had a warm coka cola, there being no electricity to run 'fridges' in this part of the universe. Back at the D.C.'s camp, George wrote up his notes, while Tembo rounded up some dead wood and started a fire. End of day two.

Day three was consumed with the enquiries from other stations about the whereabouts of various persons, some satisfactory results. One of the sought locals lived in a kraal that was a way from the road. The Sgt ascertained that the hut required was a short walking distance from the road. Stiff from sitting in the truck, they set off for the huts. It seemed like 5 miles, in the hot sun before they got there. It was not that far, but the perspiration was running on George's face, his shirt clung to his back. In Shona, near is Dousi. Very near would be Dousi Dousi Logically thought he, on the point of being kicked for making him walk that far, would be Dousi, Dousi, damn Dousi

Little African children were running away. They had never seen a white man before. This kraal wasn't on any map that was issued. That was worth a 'browny' point in the days' log.

The women folk were working in their plots, but the men nowhere to be seen. The men were at a neighbouring kraal having a beer-drink. Seven day brew it was called. A 45 gallon drum, without a lid, was suspended over a fire. The drum was part filled with water, then corn, sugar and anything else was added. It was boiled for a few days' then allowed to cool. The gathered men sat around in a circle, with gourds made from empty dried fruit husks Often they shared the same gourd, it was passed from left to right. It was the only brew that is almost chewable depending on the level reached in the barrel. If there any left, it was distilled to make Skokian or Nipa. was really evil stuff that had them blind drunk for days. It was the stuff that caused knife fights and burning down each other's huts, when under the influence. Nipa was illegal, by the Law of the Country not just the Chief.

Here at these beer drinks, a lot of tribal things were sorted out. It was the African equivalent of an Indian Pow-Wow. Spirits could be appeased here. Pleas to the spirits for more rain, another boy child, better crops, even death anniversaries. As get together, George was to use it his advantage in the future.

On day four, it was back to the Station. George learned that Nyampanda meant in Shona, the place of

Panda. Panda was a witch doctor who travelled far and wide. Nyama can also mean meat.

Big surprises at Nyamapanda greeted them. The pioneers had arrived to install generators that would bring light and power all day long, for the whole camp. Also outside security floodlights. Another piece of news was that plans were afoot to tar the road. Wonders will never cease here. What would they think of that back home.

One of the Pioneers, a large framed light skinned, fair-haired Brit called Barry, who loved a game of 'Crib'. This card game is for those who can add up and do quick permutations of small numbers. Guy and George took on the Pioneers most nights, playing for matches. The losers buy beers. One good thing about them being there was that they left on Friday afternoons and came back on Mondays. Anyone having a weekend pass could scrounge a lift to Salisbury, both ways. Sensible evening distractions always welcome at bush stations.

The morning brought a new revelation. Gordon had finished his time there and was to be replaced. George was to be the new Prosecutor for Nyamapanda cases that went to court in Mtoko. Bud put him through his paces as a bit of training, but like a great many things in outer lying places, one has to 'wing' it. Use common sense, imagination, and some homework, beforehand.

It also meant that he did the Thursday mail and beer-run, and saw some other people. Life was looking up, just shade.

The rains had come and gone, despite the ferocity of some storms, the rains were lacking that year. It was time for a patrol up to the north of the area to Baobab Beacon, and the Mazoe River. The usual preparations were made this time accompanied by Sgt. Matambara. The road (still dirt) took us to Kotwa, where the turn-off road north was.

North of the Mazoe river, Mount Darwin's area took over, and this was bandit country, so we were both armed' as before, instructed not to go over the Mazoe bridge' under any circumstances. The T.T.L. between this and the border was the area that had suffered the Cholera epidemic. Because of our efforts during the epidemics was thought that the tribes people here maybe glad us. A drive of three hours brought us to the bridge crossing to Mt Darwin. The river here Was about a quarter of a mile wide. The river wasn't running much, huge pools in the sandy base teemed with wild life.

Up river, heading towards Baobab Beacon, an enormous pool was home to some Hippos. Lower downstream a similar pool housed crocodiles. The smaller water holes had tracks in the sand which indicated all kinds of antelope came to drink. No elephant tracks could be seen, and no big cats, but baboons had come. They were considered as vermin, as they could go through a crop of corn and rip it apart, ruining it for the farmers. There was a 50 cent bounty on their tails. After taking notes, they went back to nearest D.C. camp for the evening.

The following morning, they rose early, and took a track to the Beacon. There another amazing site greeted George. The magnificent Baobab tree is like few if any others.

The giant trunk is many yards in circumference. The branches resemble a root system more than usual branches. The Sgt told him a legend, which was this.

When God made Earth he wanted all creatures to be in harmony with each other. So He matched each tree with an animal as soul mates. The mighty Baobab resented this, and made it known. Hearing of this, God picked up the tree, turned it over and rammed it back into the ground upside down.

The Baobab can be a life saver, in the bush. With its deformed looking branch system spreading out from a single height above the trunk, it soaks up water there. This can be tapped if one knows how, and drunk straight from the tree. The fruit of the Baobab is a large green pod, like huge bloated cucumber. It has a mossy hard shell. When split open, it shows a white; hard packed;

powder, with a vine of seeds embedded in it. This is the real Cream of Tartar and is perfectly edible as such.

The cream of tartar, was brewed, then used, as an anti malarial remedy.

What was also so absolutely incredible, was that usually these trees are loners, spaced apart. Here was like a forest of them only thirty or so feet apart. On the other side of the cattle fence (what was left of it) the land dropped away to feel into Mozambique as the river headed to meet Zambezi. The fence was a mess because wild animals don't care for them, they are in their way, so eventually the fence gets pushed down.

Wild Guinea Fowl make good eating in the right conditions. While on the way back from Baobab Beacon, a flock crossed the road in front of the vehicle. 'Stop'

George cried, as it was the Sgt driving then. Getting out he grabbed a shotgun and went after them. They were pecking and choosing about thirty yards away. Just as George got a sight along the shotgun's barrel they jumped up and flapped away for another thirty yards. George followed as quietly and stealthily as he could.

At thirty yards he took aim. The cunning blighters took off again. George was not going to be messed about with by a Guinea Fowl. He strode back to the truck and got out his 7.62. It would blow a hole in the bird, but that wasn't going to deter him.

He crept to within 60 yards again, and took aim. 'Got him!' Matambara went and collected it. They would eat it that night. It would be tough because it should hang for a couple of days. However, they didn't have a couple of days.

After making some notes for the report, they returned to the D.C.'s Camp. No sign of humans activity up there. With those huge trees, the indigenous couldn't farm that land, it was too far from the kraals. May be the two of them, were the first people at that desolate spot for ages.

The following day, they had to go and seek out the kraal head. It was necessary to gauge their feeling, and discover any bandit activity. The kraal-head near the Mazoe River had not seen or heard any comings or goings of bandits, but was very concerned about the baboons. They had come and spoiled some of the crops. They grab a head of corn on the shoot, rip it off, bite it, and then discard it, leaving as quickly as they had come.

The local Africans were defenceless against them. The Sgt went to the truck and picked out the fire-arms. The two police went down the embankment to the river. Looking up along the tree line beside the banks, a troop a baboons could be seen. George lined up a shot and fired. He hit one full in the chest and it clutched its front and fell, tumbling down the slope to the river. George was reminded of the guy with the white hat, shooting a 'baddy' from the window over the saloon, and the way the stunt man made a meal of it.

This time the kraal head was going to make a meal of it. They hadn't had meat for a few weeks, and the 50 cent bounty would but him a 25lb bag of sadsa.

The last port of call was at a mine. The sparse, grass filled dirt road, ran up hill towards a bedraggled hut, near a hole in the hill top. Smoke was coming out of the tin pipe on top of the corrugated steel roof. The rest was built of wooden planks, with a window to the front.

The knocks on the door, were answered by a White man, starting to go grey in the unshaved whiskers. Dressed for work not for entertaining. His narrow and lined face, made him look older, but he was only in his forties. 'Whiskey' Thomas introduced himself. George did likewise and was invited in.

'How come you are in the T.T.L. working?' from George.

'Well, I have a prospectors licence and permission from D.C. This mine was worked some years ago, then just left, so I am seeing if it worth re-opening. It would be local labour, but it depends on the yield'.

'What's here to be mined?'

'Kyanite. Here have at look at these crystals'.

'Whiskey' showed George, a clear, slightly bluish pair of crystals. They were only small and not as symmetrical as perfect pieces, of course the first he'd ever seen.

'What is Kyanite used for? What would it be worth? How much would you need?'. Questions bubbled out of his mind.

Well Kyanite has little heat expansion co-efficient. They use it with other minerals for high voltage insulators and in car spark plugs

'Could this place do that?'

'The commercial viability isn't up to me George. I'm just the guy they send to find out. Want some tea?'

He taught a tea bag to swim in luke-warm water, added some condensed mild, and offered it. George politely took and drank the mixture.

'Well the best of luck to you 'Whiskey'. I may see you around some day.

'Cheers mate. I'm back to Salisbury tomorrow, you never know'.

They drove on the Morosi dam. Here again a D.C.'s rest camp, not visited for ages, stood by a dam on a small tributary to the Mazoe. The water was getting a bit stagnant in the dam. It was a bit creepy, with thick foliage round three sides. The access side was open, even the spillway of the dam was nearly blocked by vegetation. It was gloomy and dank.

That evening, the mosquitoes came in force. It was as if 633 squadron was buzzing around their cots, fortunately covered in netting. When George swatted one, it was the size of a horse fly. If these sods got their noses into a living human arm, they would pick it up and carry it home for the family. Eventually sleep came after trying innumerable positions keeping flesh away from the side of the net. Mosquito probes could get like a monkey's arm, grabbing for a banana through the cage bars.

The following day started badly. The land Rover would not start. The radio worked, so they called up and then waited for 'Gasha' to come to the rescue. Four hours later, his grinning face appeared and the mechanics magic wand waved. Back in action. The dank place had dampened the points, nothing serious. The only thing left to do, was to get back to Nyamapanda and a decent cup of tea.

Tea wasn't the only item on the menu. While George had been away, some events had taken over. That week, as the convoy had gone through to Salisbury, Jani and Ollie had done their paperwork, and left it on their desk for a break. They said that a breeze had sprung up, and blown the paperwork onto the floor.

'Nubbin', who was quite well grown by now, had wandered into their office. Seeing a change of diet from grass to paper, he set about the paperwork. Janu and

Ollie had returned to the office to see the remains and the evidence of 'Nubbins' snack. They had then radioed Salisbury, for the convoy to be intercepted and the paperwork redone. They had to blame a freak blast of wind, and claimed that the papers were blown back across the border into Mozambique where they could not retrieve them. Salisbury would not have been very impressed by that excuse, but they could hardly tell the truth.

The bar-be-que was on the following Sunday. 'Nubbin' had already been executed. He was roasted, starting early in the day, ready for a late Sunday lunch, served with chips and beer. A fine passing for a nice goat.

Thursday was Mtoko day for George now, he was getting proficient at being Public Prosecutor and the day away from Nyamers was good.

The cases them selves did not requires 'Rumpole' of the Old Bailey. The A.P: had made arrests of Tribesmen brewing Nipa, which really smelled fould. Some times the cases been brought by the D.C. Office would have checked on the contour ridges on the land, and if not maintained, bring a case to Court. As Public Prosecutor George still had to deal with the case, and bring it to conclusion.

There was never a really sinister case for him, to cut his teeth on, but for confidence, responsibility and experience it did him plenty of good.

The Mtoko Hotel did a tasty lunch. After Court, George picked up the mail, did the shopping, and ate. The Land Rover rook took eight crates of beer exactly, so the run black was slow on a corrugated road. It wouldn't do for any bottles to jump off the roof, en route.

Every bush station was its own dispensary. Along with the anti malarial pills were all kinds of medicines for, making one go to the loo, or stopping one go. Some of the A.P. also went to a local Witch Doctor for some of Both Worlds. If the milk of magnesia didn't do it, the bark would.

One day, an African came in. He had been watching what happened, when the top of a paint aerosol was depressed. Black spray was emitted, and he got it full in the face. The paint was only shade darker than he was, so it barely showed.

An old report was re-opened, when the station received a radio message that a missing child had been found, and was being returned here. About 7 months previously. Two young African boys had been herding goats down by the Inyamzizi River. They were 8 and 9 years old, half brothers. They had both disappeared. The goats had been found, unattended.

Speculation about wild animals taking them, created searches. Hunts for animal spore were set up, even out onw tracker 'George' was used. The tracker known as

'George' was diminutive man of four feet ten inches. He was reputed to able to track a snake over rock. However nothing was found. No clothing, tracks signs of a scuffle; nothing. The children had gone.

Now one was alive and coming back. He had been found wandering, across the river in North Inyanga. He had spent a few months at Mission station there while his exhausted body recovered. Then to the Police, enquires made and half the problem solved. What about the other one? With Sgt Malambara P.O. George and couple of other Constable, went to the child's kraal, to question him, and re trace events of the initial disappearance.

The child's story was that he and the other lad had been abducted, by a single African man, whom he knew, and identified. They had been taken across the river, and to the kraal of a witch doctor, which he didn't know or could identify in any way. He had been released by the abductor and had wandered around for many days not knowing where he was, until, by chance came across the Mission.

The abductors' name was Solomon, and he was a local man living not far away.

George sent off the two constable to go get him, and get him they did. Four Police Officers, once accused, a child and its mother, headed for Nyamapanda Police

Station. Statements had to be taken, and a lot more questions asked, this time of the accused.

Solomon knew he was in deep trouble, and told the Police this story.

He had been asked to abduct one child. The child had to be old enough to walk, but not reached puberty. He was to take the child to the witch doctor in North Inyanga. He would return after the witch doctor had issued him with his instructions. The witch doctor, slew the child, and took his heart and his liver out. He told Solomon to take the rest of the child and throw in it the river for the crocodiles, which he did. He was then to release the other child. He had been told only to bring one. The child was expected to die, alone in the bush anyway.

He was to take the liver and the heart back to the case of new store that was being built, bury the heart at the front, and the liver at the back of the building. This would make new business flourish and make the owner a rich man. Solomon was not the owner. So who had set all this up.

The name of the man who had first gone to the witchdoctor, been told what was required, and paid Solomon to do this. It took a long while with him to extract the name, because it was the son of an already wealthy powerful man.

'His name is Mupate, his is from Mtoko, his father is the man who owns several stores in that area. Get on the radio to Mtoko, find him, and bring him in'. Such were the Member-in-Charge' words to Bud. Guy had had the last session with Solomon and had delivered the goods. Mutape was duly arrested and brought int. During the time that the radio was sent, and Mutape apprehended a lot of back ground word had been done. Mutape had three wives, and at first they were hazy about dates and places where he was at the salient times.

The A.P. were sent out to find people, check and double check the statements, until a pattern emerged, and the net tightened on Mutape.

This kind of murder, especially without a body, and just a child witness, depended on a lot more. The calendar of events had to be spot on, so too did the statement of Solomon.

George had left Nyamapanda when finally the case was heard in Salisbury High Court. It seems that this Solomon was not so wise. Death penalties were handed out to the two men. The witch doctor was never found Bud received a commendation on the case he produced and rightly so.

For nine months George had been in Nyamers, it was time to move again. He was ordered to Salisbury. Not Marandellas for his new posting. He was on his way to Matabeleland in the south of Rhodesia for a whole new beginning. He was given a beer-mug engraved with 'Nubbin' to commemorate his posting. He had been the first P.O: to do nine months there. He had been in the Country just a year.

FROM
NYAMAPANDA
TO DETT.

Having packed all his bags and paid his bar-bill. It was 'Goodbye' time. Even Tembo was bit sad. He had his hut built and was pretty grateful for that, but life goes on. He would get a job with the replacement P.O.

The first 'leg' of the trip, was to Mtoko by Land-Rover. Form there he was getting a lift with one of the P.O.'s there that had a car, and was going in to Salisbury on transfer too.

They got into Salisbury at 14.00 hrs and made their way first to the Central Police Oficcers, for travel warrants to their destinations. Receiving them, they had a bite of lunch before splitting up to go their separate ways. George was to get off the overnight train to Bulawayo, his colleague was off to Kariba, in his own transport. Shaking hands, and mutual 'Good lucks', they each went their way. George was taken to the Railway Station in a police car.

Being alone, George wasn't too sure about leaving his kit and going to any refreshment facilities that there may be on board the train. It was not so much his own things, but getting a consignment of uniform stuff stolen, would not be appreciated. He brought some snacks and soft drinks on the platform to tide him through. He found a compartment and settled down for the night trip south.

Salisbury Central had obviously sent a radio message on to Bulawayo because he was met by a P.O. and car, on arrival. He unloaded his bags from the train and with his hands full, followed the driver of this courtesy car to where it had been illegally parked. Police cars can do that.

Told to report to an Inspector, he waited in an anti room for twenty minutes and was at last called for. While standing to attention, he was told that his move to Matabeleland was to improve his knowledge of the Country. As a single man, being shipped around from station to station was quite normal. One just had to get used to it.

He had time get some lunch, and then he was to return to the railway station and board the afternoon train to Victoria Falls, alighting at Dett. He was given a rail warrant, and that was that.

Taking all of his 'Impasha', Bulawayo Central arranged for a car to take him to the railway station.

He was on his way to Dett, which was on the rail link to Victoria Falls. That was a much as he knew about Matabeleland. It was going to be another long day. Having not had a lot of sleep, since leaving Nyamapanda, the journey was getting tiresome.

From the extreme north east of the Country to the south-west. It could hardly have been a more distant change of Stations.

It is about 250 miles from Bulawayo to Dett, and passes along one of the world's longest straight stretches of railway track. Other than in Australia and Siberia, where there are longer straight sections of line. From the bridge over the river at Gwai it is approximately 110 miles. Seventy miles of which is in a direct line. It was not a very quick journey despite that, as the train does not pick up much speed before Gwai. All the small stations along the way are serviced like a bus route. It was very late in the day when George arrived.

At the Railway station, a European Railway Police Officer phoned to the Police Station to provide transport for him.

Sgt Chiratidzo came and picked him up. He was in Dett.

DETT.

D ett was principally a Railway town. After the
construction of the line in the 1920's, Rhodesia
Railways had to have centres for taking on water for
the steam engines. Enormous open caste coalmines,
just to the north at Wankie, provided the other basic
requirement for the engines. The town grew as the
railways system developed, with their own Police, crew
change; and mechanical requirements.

Housing development for married employees
became essential, naturally followed by schools.

The B.S.A. Police similarly increased in size, and
the Post consisted of a married Member-in-Charge, a
Section Officer and three P.O.'s. The African Police
section, had two Sergeants and the Constables, some of
these having married quarters too.

The area of control, was difficult to define. The
Wankie National Park, was south west of the railway

line, to the Botswana border. The road from Bulawayo to Victoria Fall ran parallel to the border inland from the railway, in a north-westerly line. The National Park covered an area of 14,600 square kilometers, the size of Belgium. In essence it was controlled and the responsibility of National Parks, a Government department. Liaison with the National Park (N.P.) personnel therefore, superceded internal interests.

The space between the railway and the road, became private hunting areas. Any wild life the crossed the line , could be hunted, under licences from the D.C. and N.P: depending on their assessment of specie numbers. Not all of the space was private, as the town took up a large amount, and needed to expand more. To the southern edge there was some T.T.L.

The road from Dett was half a mile to the cross roads. The main highway being two of the arms, the other being a road going north of Kamativi and Binga. Binga was on the banks of Zambezi, now part of lake Kariba. There was a large Tin Mine at Kamativi. There was another Police Post at Binga, so Dett's area didn't reach that far.

The town of Dett had evolved much like Marandellas, but smaller, and served very few inhabitants not connected to the railway. Some commercial business proprietors, Game Rangers, Teachers, and of course, the Police, lived there. The bungalows and plots were more modest than Marandellas and quite a number were detached housing for those without families. They were owned by Rhodesia Railways, and like the Police, the employees could be re-posted elsewhere.

The town boasted a Tennis Club, which was the sole centre of recreation, for all the European inhabitants. Most Sundays saw a gathering of the fitter residents, play in afternoon competitions. In the evenings it was a very hospitable place for a beer, and talk to other people who were not of their own ilk.

The Police Camp, had its station, single ground floor, gardens in front with flag pole. Several rooms inside, being offices for the Member-in-Charge, the S.O, and armoury, and interrogating rooms and cells. A bungalow behind, housed the single S.O: and P.O.s. Another building was for the A.P. and behind that a football pitch and a rifle range. The whole area was so flat, between the main road and the border, expansion by Government Departments was easy.

The S.O. was the first to greet George's arrival. Graham Goode was a Scot. He just made six feet tall, had a mature, solid build and aged about 28 years. Clean Shaven and light brown hair, regulation cut (of course).

He had been in the Force in Scotland and had come out five years ago. They shook hands and exchanged identities warmly. George could meet the inspector, who was M.I.C. the following day. Being prepared for a new arrival, Graham had laid on a 'bat-man' for George. 'Pencil' was old African, who walked at a pace, which a tortoise could match. Slightly built (meaning thin) he had worked before at the Camp. George thought that Graham was being rather charitable to old boy, but 'Go with the flow'.

The other P.O.'s were Danny Van De Merve, an 19-year-old from Bulawayo and nick Easterby, whose parents had a farm a Gokwe in the Midlands area.

Danny was very tall and thin, the Africans had nicknamed him 'Giraffe' behind his back. Nick was quiet and studious, regular build and 20 years old. He want to make a career in the Police.

Inspector Arthur Grainger was the Boss. If I wasn't done his way. It was done again until it was. If anything was not to his satisfaction, a rebuke was forthcoming. In his fifties, a large man with a slightly imperious attitude. It could be conceivable that he had been passed over for promotion, this was as good as he was going to get, George didn't expect to get on to well with this man.

Another major characters of the Mess was 'Jumbo', He was Graham's dog. A cross of setter, Pointer and mastiff, he had a light livery colour, and was the most intelligent fog George had ever come across before or since. Graham could 'tell' 'Jumbo' in the Charge Office to go and get P.O: Simpson. 'Jumbo' would go to the Mess, where George was, he would 'woof', then gently take George's hand in his mouth and lead him back to the station. 'Jumbo' was marvelous and went on patrols with Graham.

'Stables and radio were exactly the same as every other station, the only difference was the call sign. That morning a road patrol was scheduled to familiarize George with some of the geography of the area. He was to be accompanied by Sgt Ndhlovu.

The drive took them to the Private Hunting Areas where customary introductions were made, then a brief run through of what happens at each. The business of just hunting in the bush took on whole new dimensions. Not only were wealthy clients kept contented with their 'prizes' but the bi-products had to generate money too. The dead animals had to be carefully skinned, and the skins tanned for sale. The meat was properly butchered and used for food for the Arican workers and the making of 'Biltong' for commercial sale.

'Biltong' is a raw meat. The meat is cut into strip, dipped in a brine of salt and vinegar, and any private additive the Company may have. Then it is hung out to dry, until the state of hardness required, is reached. Packaging it was done Bulawayo for commercial distribution. George was given a few sticks of Kudu, which as game meat has no fat, and is quite tasty.

They crossed the railway, into the National Park and drove beside the tracks on a dirt service road. While George's concentration on he road, was distracted, the backside of a tall full grown male Giraffe backed across the way. Slamming on the brakes, no collision took place, but who was the more shaken George or the Giraffe. It was hard to tell with the animal loping off, and George sweating. The first he had seen a non zoo giraffe and he nearly runs into it. The backside was a few feet higher than the truck though.

He let the Sgt drive from then on, just so he could watch all around him, as Impala and other game browsed the bushes, or ran off on their approach. There were hundreds of Zebra miling around too. Another New World was opening up for him.

As long as George stayed at Dett he was to see more unforgettable sights. On one patrol, a car had stopped in front of his land Rover, and he could see over the top of it. From the left side of the road came a couple of lion cubs, then a magnificent sandy grey lioness, whose nose was about over the 9ft wide road, while its tail was starting to cross. The lioness took a look around and saw the vehicles. She gave them such a disdainful expression, as if to say 'You're just Humans, I'm a Lioness'.

One evening the P.O.'s had been for a drink at the Tennis Club. Nick had a car so they had gone in that. As they returned to the Mess, a left sweeping turn had to be negotiated through a gate to the parking area. As the light swung round large target appeared in the middle of the football pitch. It was the rear end of a water-buck. It had crescent shaped white markings on each rear cheek, centring just below the base of the tail.

The first serious investigation assigned to him, was a hit and run accident at Kamativi Mine. It had taken place at night. A car had hit an African pedestrian, knocking him off the side the road. There were no street lights. There was no side pavement or pedestrian walk way. The Mine had its own hospital, where the African had been taken. Sadly, the injured body was not found until morning light and the African had died of his injuries over night.

Two constables went up with George to help with the accident report. This Mine had hundreds of employees, a lot with cars. Most of those cars had damaged wings, fenders and lights. Trying to find the vehicle was going to be bad enough, let alone get the responsible owner/driver. The Mine Manager was as helpful as he possibly could have been. Few if any of the housed engineers go out, and then only to each's home for social evening. With work going on at the 24-7, the processing and shifting of the ore, early to bed early rise was the watchword.

Of the African workers, a few had vehicles. However then the nature of living here and having to get back to their T.T.L. for any Time Off, many had hidden cars. The directions of travel of the vehicle in question, was in itself misleading, going virtually away from the mine, towards Binga. That was even less help.

All that could be done, was done. Without any witnesses as to even a type of car, when it happened, the enquiry went nowhere. Even Mr Grainger conceded that. The Mine however was interesting, as it had a progressive attitude towards training its' workers for future middle management and engineering jobs. It also has a school where two charming young single ladies taught.

Betty and Janice, were the academic versions of Patrol Officers. Having finished College and graduated as Teacher, the Education Authority sent them to their own 'Siberia' Kamativi Mine.

Betty's hair was dark brown, with hazel eyes. She was five feet five inches tall and was a medium build, carrying a few extra pounds. Janice was slim and had mousy coloured hair. She stood five six inches in height and wore a lot of trinkets and baubles. They got on well together, but had nothing to offer to George's investigation.

Living on the very edge of a vast natural area, meant that raw Africa was all around. Graham found this to his cost. He was preparing the rifle range for training shoot. He checked out where the shooters were to be positioned, 200 yards from the targets. Pacing out ground towards the butts, his mind was on his check list. Stepping down to the metal hut, below ground level, he failed to notice a large cobra. With its natural camouflage, and stealth of movement, it watched Graham get nearer. Graham was engrossed with getting the hut keys from his pockets. He was perspiring quite a bit and raised his right arm to wipe sweat from his brow.

The cobra spat. The venom flew across the air towards Graham's eyes. A movement from pure instinct, or was it the end of the wipe, that Grahams head turned. The venom hit his temple, and ran down the side of his face. He ran back up the steps and fled the scene.

Back at the Mess he threw himself into the bathroom. He ran the shower full on cold, and faced the downpour, washing away the poisonous spittle. He was still shaking when, alerted by his entrance, Danny came to see what was wrong. They drew shotguns from the armoury and went back down the butts. Caution dictated the search pattern, but the cobra was long gone.

That incident caused some concern around the town. Graham had quite a few free beers on the strength of the tale, when it was told and retold. Snakes in the garden was not a rare occurrence in Dett, but snaked usually retreated from man, not start a fight.

That weekend, Graham and George did a road patrol, to the Southern Sun Safari Lodge, near Main Camp. They met by chance with Jim Popplewell, a Game Ranger. He was a good looking, outdoor man, he had blond hair, unkempt with wind and sweat. His build was the like of a tough athlete.

The Safari Lodge was a modern five star Hotel built in an arc, about 100 metres from a large natural pool. Mornings and evenings, the residents and guests could watch the Game come and drink. From that Distance the animals would not be scared or hindered or feel threatened.

Jim told his companions about a Game Ranger that got bit over-confident with a family of elephants. The man's name was Johnny Ayce, and it was thought among Ranger circles that he was was showing off to some ladies.

The story goes, that Johnny was with a party of tourist and some elephants with young came near. Johnny told the tourists to stay where they were, but he himself crept nearer and nearer. Danny was quite close to a calf, when Mummy elephant took umbrage. The Cow Knocked Johnny down with her trunk, and then knelt on him. She then pulled him limb from limb and threw the dismembered parts all around. A salutary warning to all who get to close to wild animals with their young.

Danny was leaving. He had been posted to Pandamatenga, which was up on the Botswana border lower down the Zambezi than Victoria Falls. It is called the 'Panhadle' where four countries, nearly fve, meet. Rhodesia, Zambia, Botswana and South West Africa come to point, and Angola is not very far away, upriver. It was not a very happy place for fun and entertainment, though great for wild life spotting.

In the Ndabele language, Matenga meant place of. So this revered witch doctor must have travelled along the Zambezi, as it was, all around Rhodesia. From Nyamapanda to Pandametanga.

He was being replaced with a new recruit. This recruit was part of a new Government Scheme to boost man power by having National Service P.O:s No one knew what to expect.

He turned out to be a decent young man, whose father happened to be a Senior Officer in the Police, Geoffrey Dickens was average height with dark hair, Self confident nearly to the point of arrogance. Possible because of his father's rank. His common sense seemed to be a bit off key, when screams were heard from the kitchen one day. Geoffrey had found a puff adder in the grounds, killed it, and put it in the deep freeze. The Africans had opened lid and found it staring at them.

Graham asked him what the 'blank' he was thinking about. He said he was going to dissect it later, as it looked like a pregnant female. The following day was a Sunday. Graham and George took the opportunity to do a road patrol to Main camp and hand it over to the Game Rangers, who may find it interesting. George met Jim Popplewell, the Ranger. The three had a beer together and chatted about the rains and general topics.

George's next patrol was to be four day trip. Up to Kamativi, over the Gwai River, then round to Lubimi. He was to take Sgt Ndlovu.

Day one of the journey was up the tar road to Kamativi and do a couple of enquiries on the way. The Sgt explained his name. Ndlovu was the Sindabele word for Elephant. Such christenings were done, in the parent's hope, that the child would inherit the characteristic of the beast. He would be proud, strong and noble. Other names such as Ncube were the same. Ndluvu spoke Sindabele, of course, English and B'tonka. The B'tonka were a tribe, which lived in the area we were going to. They had lived on both sides of the Zambezi, but now the dam at Kariba had formed tha lake, the tribe was split. He said that they were primitive compared to other Tribes.

That evening George had re-acquainted himself with the young lady teachers, and stayed the night at their bungalow at the mine. It was so pleasant to have female company again. He especially got on with Betty and they made plans to get together when they had mutual time-off. Janice had a car, which could ferry them to Dett whenever a suitable time could be arranged.

The patrol resuming on day two, further up the road towards Binga, but not as far. The land here was much higher than Dett. They were going up on the central Rhodesian plateau. The river Gwai was down a densely forested valley, and then up again on the other side. A tributary of the Gwai was down into another valley, not so steep this time and more northerly. Here they stopped at a B'tonka kraal.

The men folk sat around looking totally bored with life. Very dark skin and quite for Africans, they dressed in wrap-arounds like sarongs. The distinguishing feature was a hole in the base of their noses, between nostrils. It was large enough for a small bone. If Europeans had such a hole, it would take a biro, or even a fountain pen.

Nothing much to report from them. A right turn onto a dirt road directed the Land Rover to Lubimbi.

One of the usual grinds about bush patrols, is cleanliness. It is impossible to get enough water for a shower at the end of day. Lubimbi was totally the opposite. Here, hot water bubbled up out of the ground and was chanelled to huge pool. The channel and the pool were man made. The pool was the size of a large public swimming, which it had been. A derelict hotel stood there, and the pool was part of the grounds. Maybe in the 20's or 30's one can imagine it being a Spa. An hotel featuring a full frontal veranda. Bearded settlers with pith helmets and gin and tonics. A thatched roof and a long room, festooned with stuffed animal heads. Now it was a ruin with a fabulous warm water bath, big enough to swim in. So, Swim they did, glorious luxury on a sweaty day patrol day.

Another Land rover pulled up, and out jumped another pair of travelers, One African, one European. Johannes Potgeiter was a District Officer from the D.C.'s of food which he added to and ate from each day. 'Time for a shoot' he said. A little way south of the pool was a pan that the pool water drained into. Surrounded by grass and weeds it was good for ducks.

'If we can bag a duck, it will go into the pot. It won't be ready to eat just yet though. Got to hang it a bit.' He said.

George took a shotgun and followed him through the grass to the pan. Not a duck in sight. In fact nothing to shoot at, at all. Glumly they went back, but shared their dinner anyway. The old mattresses, what was felt of them, were alive with living creatures. There were solid levels, like tables, that were fine to lie on. Patrol life is like that.

The third day came, and a plan that George had buzzing in his head for some time, was to be realise. Throught the previous days, while stopping at kraals, the Sgt had left word of a beer-drink for kraal heads, at a beer hall in Dhalia on the Gwai River, lower down. The African town ship there had a Chibuku hall, where the State Beer was supplied. George organised a large pot of sadsa, and some meat. A Patrol allowance of two dollars and change per day was paid. For just a few dollars, all the walking to kraals and individual chats, were to be combined into an Indaba for all the locals.

One by one they drifted in. Soon about twelve heads were there. Once seated, in a big circle, the beer was produced and the food. The formalities of thank and the passing around of the chibuku started. As host, George drank first and passed the gourd to his right. Sgt Ndluvo had to do all the talking, which was fine, but George had to stay there to show respect. He occasionally had to promise to bring a matter to some one attention. And wrote it in his report.

That night they went back to Lubimbi, for a swim and a rood, although decrepit, over their heads. It had been a success, and saved a lot of time and effort.

The final day dictated a drive to the railway line, and follow it back to Dett. This was not the most direct route, but it showed their faces, and a Police presence in a outlying areas.

Where the dirt road met the railway line, there was a siding, and a train pulled into it. The Locomotives were a train spotters dream. A huge; shiny; Beyer Garett loco with front water tank. George knew the driver from Dett's tennis club, so he climbed up the cab for a chat. The reason they were there, was that a special train was coming down from Victoria Falls. They had to wait until it had passed, being only a single track stretch of line. It was enthralling having that powerful locomotive at ones' control. Only a handful of levers were required, to send the monster that lived on coal and water, on its way. Sadly George had to be on his way, in a humble truck. Back to base.

The best news for a long while came George's way the following day. Penny had finished work at Bindura Hospital and was taking some time of before starting her new job in pharmaceuticals. He had the weekend off, so suggested she fly over and they tour the National park. She O.K.'d the idea.

George borrowed Nick's car and drove to the Main Camp airport. There were only a couple of flights in or out per day. The Air Traffic Controller had to blow a loud wind a horn while the 'plan was approaching, to scare of birds and other animals from the runaway. She was amongst a group of visitors, but easy to spot, in jeans and neck. The sun shone through her hair making it appear to be a brown halo. All smiles and hugs they greeted each other. It was still quite early, and they had a whole day together.

They passed and saw all kinds of 'game', until they saw ahead, a herd of elephants, approaching a water hole. Stopping the car, some way back they sat and watched. A male bull replete with a pair of three ft long, white, tusk, and waterhole, as the smaller bull, the females (cows) and the calves drank at the water. The calves played with each other, the cows sucked and sprayed themselves. This continued for several minutes, until another bull relieved the guard, and took station by the road. The first bull drank and showered, and then led the family off into the bush, as another family, that of the second bull, took advantage of the waterhole. This continued for six families. The youngest of the calves chased some guinea fowl that had the temerity to want to share the water with them. It was fantastic sight.

Sadly, no big cats were to be seen that day, but it was enjoyed to the full. They chatted and laughed their way through, until it was time for her to go back. After a drink at the Safari Lodge it was time for 'Good-byes'. Best wishes to the family, hugs, kisses, and promises. It was evident to them both however, that with the great distance and time barriers between them, that a binding arrangement was nearly impossible. They mutually agreed to stay good friends, but she and he had lives to lead. It was by far the best for each and both, that this be so. It was agreed. The return to the Police Camp seemed rather empty.

One of the strangest duties of the S.O. and P.O.s in Dett, was that of Driving Examiners. Aspiring drivers, first had to learn the Rhodesian Highway Code. Passing a verbal test on that, they got a provisional licence and could take driving lessons. A driving school run by an African, provided tuition.

On the lighter side of testing, was that the Africans learned all the words of the book, but didn't really understand the essence of it. The book stated that in the even of an accident, one should not leave the scene, but if there was death, protect the corpse. George asked one lad 'What is a corpse' He replied 'It is a wood in England'. One African lad was willing to 'piggy.back' a victim with a broken leg to hospital, all be it that the nearest hospital was miles away. The sequence of colours of traffic lights was always changing. To top it all, if anyone passed their licence here, they could drive in Salisbury, or possibly even Johannesburg with it. That would be dangerous.

On one occasion while taking a driving test, George banged his clipboard on the dash to signal an emergency stop. The driver put one hand out of the window (in order to stop the following wagon train). The other hand yanked up the hand brake. Now he had no hands left, he stood on the foot brake, but forgot the clutch. 'Sorry son, not this time'.

Graham got so tired of it, he impounded the Driving school car for poor braked, which took care of that for a while. George had failed one of the European ladies in Dett, for her reversing. He had the 'micky' taken out of him at the tennis club. She was the overweight wife of one of the Railways Police. Her husband couldn't thank him enough, and bought George a few beers.

The rains were over. The skies sunny and cloudless all day, every day. It was time for a patrol of the border between Dett and Botswana. Wankie park was the northern tip of the Kalahari Desert. After the dense growth of the immediate area, it thinned out as one travelled south. Some of the river in the Dett area flowed south to the great pans in Botswana, which like the Okavanga were bird and 'game' sanctuaries. Being just after the rains, nobody could tell in advance, what condition the tracks would be in. 'Game' trails and fire clearings would be overgrown. The elephant would have left six inch deep footprints in the mud. 'Go and check it out Shipman', was the order.

Sgt Chiratidzo was to accompany George. The Rover was packed with supplies, especially water. The water they would come across would not be fit to drink. It would have been used by the 'Game' or have bilharzia. (A water born tropical disease). They took coarse salt and tobacco, to trade with the tribesmen in the northern Kalahari, should they meet any. They took fire arms mainly for protection, and blankets.

The first part of the journey took them through the National Park to Sinamatella Camp, then on the Robins Camp. Here are the bases for the Park Ranger to watch and count the 'Game', then on to assess 'culling' and foliage deprivation. At Robins Camp, the Rangers told George that border was identifies by small cement markers. Thought they doubted that these could be seen in the new growth.

A track through a cutting, following a small river, took them, the distance it should have been to the border, No lumps of cement were visible. The grass was high but yellowing. To cross the stream they found a muddy ford, but half way across, the half-shaft broke. They were stuck. Radio was messages were sent, but it was several hours before help came. An old pick-up type land rover replaced the original, which was taken back to Dett.

It was getting dark then, so they pitched a camp, a little way away from the steam, in case they disturbed animlas coming to drink at sundown.

Day two began with a cup of tea, and look around. The landscape was open and flat. There were stunted trees scattered about, which were still green. A study of the map, compass bearings and mileage, ascertained their location. They searched for border markers, but found nothing. Their heading was south-east, after re-packing they set off. Chiratidzo, who spoke Kalanga as well as Sindabele and English, was from further south. He explained that Pandamatenga meant in Sindabele, place of Panda. So this mysterious witch doctor must have travelled right across what was then open Africa. Maybe he followed the Zambesi it was dammed.

The going got really rough as they drove over elephant spoor. Deep footprints left in the ground shook every wheel as they progressed, down up, down up. George decided that they had to leave this direction to get off the elephant trial. A short distance south, the going was easier. There should be a track to follow, where previous patrols had been. Still no sign of a border marker.

Looking up, a wheeling flock of vultures, circled ahead. Driving closer, thirty or so had landed. They stopped, armed themselves, got out, and walked closer. The vultures had a wingspan of about ten to twelve feet, and bald headed. Basically cowardly birds they backed off at the approach of the two humans.

On the ground, was the carcass of an elephant. The trunk was gone, the tail; tusks; and lower legs. Skin from the belly had been removed. This was work of poachers, and their spoils. Empty tins nearby, products of South Africa, indicated that the poachers had come from the south. The animal had been shot first, then carved up.

The land now was more open. It was vast panorama of grass, bending in the breeze, for miles around. Low and behold, a tack, heading south-east. No cement lumps though. To the left (north) of the track, it began to thicken up with trees and even a few Baobab trees. Consulting the map, 'Cream of tartar' pan indicated. They camped there for the night, after radio schedule in to Dett, with their location.

Just after dawn, the radio schedule brought no new instructions so with Sgt Chiratidzo driving now, they followed the track heading south east. It was still tree lined on the north side, but open on the south. A vehicle approached which was most unusual, here of all places.

It was a patrol of Police from Botswana. They stopped exchanged greetings, and informed the B.S.A. Police that they were about 50 yards inside their Country. They gave Chiratidzo directions, to go to their Camp, which was near, turn left so we would be back in Rhodesia.

At the camp they were stopped. Their Man in Charge wanted authorization from Francistown before he would let them through. Despite explanations, they were disarmed, and stood away from the vehicles. Basically they had been arrested 50 yards into the wrong country.

Later that day, they learned that they would be taken under escort to Francistown and detained. No opportunity to use the radio was granted.

At Francistown, the two were held in custody until the evening, and again under escort taken to the railways station. They were taken by train to Gaberone. Perhaps they were going to be shot as spies. The overnight trip was uneventful. At Gaberone, it was off to the Police Headquarters. Being a British citizen, the Embassy sent a functionary to see George. 'If in the event that I have to spend a long time here, please tell my parents'. This was the instruction he gave. What was to happen however, he learned later, that the functionary just went ahead and told the Shipmans. The message scared the pants off them. George was only to be week or so in Botswana, not lifetime.

The return journey, to Fracistown, was during the day. It enabled George to get and idea of the landscape. Boring, open, dusty and dry, was his conclusion. The towns that passed had no featured that really took ones notice. At the end of the journey, it was to the State Prison, that would keep them until the next Monday, which court day.

The Prison was perhaps the bleakest place George had seen in all of his travels. The front wall were unpainted yellow blocks. It appeared a sheer façade of gloom. The entrance door was guarded by Prison Officers with rifles. Had they a 'shoot to kill policy' for escapes?

Inside, the formalities began. There were forms to sign and pockets to be emptied. The paperwork was minimal, possibly because many of the inmates were sadly illiterate. The patrol food was there, as well all, except the rifles.

The Sgt and the P.O. were dispatched to cells.

Through the reception area, iron gate opened out into a bare courtyard. One side of the courtyard, he was in was the Administration block. The other three sides were cellblocks that looked like brick barns, joined by high walls. To his left were three such barns. Across ahead of him were two more. To his right another three.

The walls of the cells were twenty feet high, with a slightly arched roof, for when it rained.

The fronts of the building were broken only by a door, which was entry or egress. A small dormer window was high up over the door.

Inside, the cells were bare cement walls, the door at one end, opened out into the courtyard. A window, high up in the opposite wall complemented the one over the door. A bucket of water was provided at one end and a bucket for a toilet, the other end, for night use. Few tried the water bucket, it case some one had got confused.

The bed was a two-inch thick cushion, the size of a large sun bed lounger, covered in plastic. One pillow and one blanket were allowed. No linen was issued. Ten people per cell, five on each side. George was the only European in the whole prison. They did however, let him use up the tinned rations that he had for his patrol food.

Day to day was totally boring. A reveille at sin in the morning, taking turns for the ablutions, which were dreadful, compared to what George was used to. The loo was a hole in the ground. A metal plate surrounded the hole so 'overspill' could be hosed off. The washing area consisted of sinks and cold taps. All grey metal, and solidly fixed on a table about three feet off the ground. They were situated in recess of the Admin block wall. That meant that there was no plumbing in any area near the cell block.

The inmates just lounged around all day in the sun. the doors to the cells were left open, if anyone wanted shade. There was nothing to do at all, except talk to one another.

Meals were taken in the yard on metal plates that were issued at the time. A slab of Sadza for each, and maybe some sort of watery meat or vegetable with it. George and the Sgt were allowed to use his tins, from the patrol rations. It was not uncommon for families to being food from outside, to compliment the Prison Fare.

At the end of these gruelling days, at six in the evening, it was back inside the cells. An electric light burned until nine., after which it was total darkness.

The African are great singer. One night, from a distant cell came a lament. Each person has their own verse, if they wish. The chorus was 'Sabuseeling, Sabuseeling Sabuseeling'. An African next George explained and translated as the verses came over. One voice sang that his cattle had been washed away in a flash flood. The chorus meant, that is gone, past, water under the bridge, not forgotten, but over. Another sang of the death of his children. So it went on, each prisoner that sang, had his own sorrow. It was a philosophy that hey all shared. Remember, but move on with your life.

Court day dame, and George and the Sgt were charged with entering the Country illegally, by not reporting to the authorities at the border. Importing arms illegally. It made them sound like a gun-runners. Rhodesia had sent a lawyer, to represent them. George tried to accept full responsibility as he was the Senior

Officer of the two. The Judge didn't seem very moved by it. They were bailed out, to return in a month. Bail was set at 300 dollars. The Lawyer paid, and they were released. After thanking the lawyer profusely, the truck was returned to them. Other personnel items, less the rifles (which were evidence) they packed, and drove back to Rhodesia comfortably, on the main tar road.

When they re entered at Plumtree, the member in Charge sent for George, and greeted him warmly. Never had such a thing happened before, and it had caused a real stir, the they should have been treated so. The relations between border Police had deteriorated. Formerly, Botswana Police and the B.S.A. Police had been mutually investigated. The incident had been in the newspapers, and very high levels of Government had been asking questions of the Botswana leaders.

The Rhodesian Railway drivers had wanted to strike. The railways go through to Botswana, on the line from Bulawayo to Gaberone. George got a lot of support when he arrived back at Dett. He was glad that was over, but he still had to face the music, in a month's time.

Returning to Francistown by a more formal route, George and Sgt Chiritidzo faced the Court and were found 'Guilty' on both counts. The fine was 300 dollars, which the court already had from the bail money. They were free then to return to Rhodesia. Later on, the lawyer successfully appealed, and the verdicts over turned. They were not International criminals after all.

A bit of good news was that he had been given a weekend leave, so too had Nick, who had a car. To top this, Betty and Janice, the schoolteachers from Kamativi, were coming down. Nick and he planned a day trip to Victoria Falls with the girls.

All board for Victoria Falls and off they went. It was a two hour drive, but it flew by, as they talked and listened to George's story, first hand.

Nick and Janice sat up front, while George and Betty sat together behind, getting closer and closer, it wasn't long before their met.

The first stop was at a crocodile farm. Small, medium and large reptiles, some were for handbags, some for the wild. They were reared from their eggs until ready for what ever future was in store for them. It was all really interesting. Crocodiles were not an endangered species, so some were culled when just old enough to have their skins used for tourist purposes. Lunch was taken at the Victoria Falls Hotel. Then it was time to visit the falls itself.

The Falls have been a wonderful sight for ages. A huge cliff, where the river falls into a ravine, and hundreds of feet below, they crash and surge their way out of the rocks. The river wasn't very high, as the rains up steam had not been good that year. There were stones lodged in trees where they been carried in previous years. The spray formed rainbows that coloured the air, just above the top of the falls. The dampness allowed lush growth and orchids to flourish. It must have been the same sight the greeted Dr Livingstone on his travel across Africa. Such that he naed them after the British Queen

The Finale of day, was the cruise to Kandahar Island. A boat left the dock up stream from the Hotel, it cost only four dollars each. The cruise along the banks of the Zambezi passed elephant and hippo drinking while crocs were in search for vulnerable prey. The sun was setting over the river ahead of them. Kandahar Island, was reached and the boat turned round. The setting sun was at their backs, as they sipped a cool beer on board.

The return journey was a bonus for George, as he succeeded in getting a kiss and a cuddle from his new friend, What a memorable day.

Life at Dett continued much of a much-ness for the next two weeks, until a letter arrived from Kamitivi, suggesting another rendezvous. Betty was to borrow Janice's car on the following Sunday, and they would go out together.

She arrived as expected, and got quite excited at the prospect of touring the National Park for the day, and go Game spotting.

The sky was clear and bright, but it was not hot yet. They drove to main Camp and the Safari Lodge, and from there headed for Sinamatella. It was a tarred road, about nine feet wide.

Driving slowly, to get full advantage of all that could be seen, a lot of Wild Life was on the move. Tall Giraffes grazed in the tree branches, Impala and Kudu nibbled the grass on the ground. A family of elephant made their way parallel to the road, but far enough away not to be bothered by the presence of humans.

The stretch of food ahead was straight, as form the sky feel what looked like a stick. They stopped and looked up. High above, circled a large Hawk. Cautiously approaching the stick, it turned out to be a snake, a green mamba. The hawk had gripped it in its talons and carried it up. The snake would then be still alive and wriggling. The Hawk sees a hard surface, like a road, and drops the snake on to it, breaking its back, and killing it.

They drove away briskly, hoping the hawk would get its breakfast, without being disturbed by them.

They had lunch at Sinametella and headed back. Unfortunately there were no lions to be seen that day, but plenty of grazers and browsers.

Much later, Betty had to head for home.

Graham called George in to his office the following day. There was news. He was being transferred again.

George was once more on the move. He received a beer mug from the good burghers of Dett. This one was engraved, 'The Kalahari Kid'

On advice from Graham, he asked Pencil if he wanted to come with him.

'Yeees Boss' was the slow, drawn out reply. So off they went.

ESSEXVALE

E ssexvale was a suburban satellite town of Bulawayo. It was situated forty miles south east on a wide tarred road. Developed with bungalows, chalets, and all the trimmings of a civilised society. A far cry from what George had experienced in places like Nyamapanda.

This main road was the major highway from Bulawayo south westerly to Gwanda and on to Beit Bridge, the border crossing into South Africa.

Inspector Benny Stone was the Member in Charge. In his mid forties, Benny was South African born from Springs near Johannesburg. Thinning fair hair on top, medium height and build. A very genial and likeable man. Section Officer Stephan Miles and P.O.s Ashley Devonport and Paulus Kruger. The P.O.'s were both just eighteen and inexperienced.

Work and duties were much the same as every where else, so George settled in without fuss. It was the first

Sunday there which showed the youth of the two P.O.s In the single men's quarters, all three were lounging around but Ashley was the one who was 'on call' Paulus had invited round his young lady friend and was trying impress her. Lucy was up from Bulawayo, and had been collected by Paulus on his motor cycle.

At about 4 p.m. Paulus was to take his girlfriend out for a 'spin' on his bike. He was high spirited and ebullient. George told him not to do anything silly with her on the back of the bike.

Ten minutes later came the call to go and help him. They had fallen off just a mile away. Ashley being on call, took a land rover and went to help. Half an hour after that, they were back in the bungalow, Paulus uninjured Lucy with gash on her right thigh which had torn the skin back and exposed flesh. Ashley returned to the Charge Office to get medical help from the local services. George carried Lucy to Paulus' room and laid her downn on the bed. He helped her remove her shorts which were impeding the cleaning up of the wound. While washing the grit and dirt, with a warm water and antiseptic the two talked. George comforted her, and assured her that the wound wasn't limb threatening (he had seen a lot worse). Paulus had not experienced anything like it, and he couldn't handle it at all. Each time he came near her he was ready to retch and it disturbed her greatly.

It didn't take long for her to banish him from the room completely, She only wanted George in attendance. An ambulance arrived so they carried her to it. Lucy was taken back to Bulawayo, where her parents would be waiting. That was end of that aspiring romance.

On the other hand, George's love life took an enormous leap forwards. Penny's new job as a representative for a pharmaceutical company, had sent her down on a course in Bulawayo. She and George had a weekend off together. They made plans to do some touring together. In a hired car, they passed Essexvale down to Balla Balla and turned to Shabani and Fort Victoria destination Zimbabwe.

Kyle National Park, was home to some white Rhino. The rhino were on an island in Lake Kyle, which was reached by ferry. The ferry was a one vehicle wooden affair, which took them over and returned for the next customer. To summon the barge to collect them, raise a flag on the jetty. They crossed over the Hat water and drove slowly along a dirt road. The advice to drive slowly and carefully was well meant, as one doesn't want to excite a rhino into doing anything dramatic. These beasts can weigh a couple of tons. Even with the tough hide and short thick legs, they can sprint short bursts of up to 30 m.p.h. The snout and horn are capable of penetrating the thin metal of a car. Respect them.

One hundred yards away a tail swished, soon they saw their first rhino. They stopped and just watched as it browsed. A magnificent, pale skinned animal tank of a Creature. It must have been six feet high to the shoulder and ten feet long. Staying away Possibility of getting nearer. They had seen a beauty fairly close up. That was enough.

There was an abundance of Zebra, chewing their way to the waters edge. Donkeys in pyjamas, they joked.

They stayed at a Safari Lodge that night, and resumed their exploration after breakfast. This day was for the Great Zimbabwe Ruins.

Great Zimbabwe is one of the many unexplained wonders of Africa. Great walls of dry stone, three feet wide at the base and several feet high. There stands a solid tower some thirty feet high of solid construction. It's use, no-one can fathom. The ruins stand in 60 acres of land Smaller stone walls, which could have been compounds for cattle or slaves are evident all over the land there.

It is surmised that early Arab traders came here for Gold, slaves or Ivory. They may have come from the Mozambique Coast through a pass in the Chimanimani Mountain range. Did they come by sea,? up the Sabi river and then smaller waterways deeper inland. can tell what they did in the 11th century. Who were those

Africans that lived there then? The Ruins are incredible feat of engineering, a thousand years old. built it? and who taught them how to build it?

Returning to Essexvale was the next phase of weekend. It was a couple of hundred miles so enough time had to be allocated. A quiet, harmonious atmosphere prevailed on the drive. The excitement of what they had seen lifted up the spirits. Then the sadness of the approaching parting of the ways. There was always the future.

Back 'in harness' at work, George's turn for a Patrol came along. He was to go south to Balla Balla, then east to the edge of the Matopas and Rhodes National Park.

He was to take with him Constable Ncube. of the Ndebele Tribe, who had 12 years experience. He was the same height as George. He had broad shoulders, built like a boxer. The Ndebele Tribe was originally from further south when Chaka was King of the Zulus.

They broke away from the Zulu under a chief called Mzilikazi, founder of the Matabele nation. They moved north and west into the Political regions of Botswana and Rhodesia. As a warrior Tribe, they defended their lands against Rhodes' Colonisation of the area. It was his son Lobengula who was to befriend the White man. Gobulawayo (Bulawayo) was Lobengula's capital.

Ncube knew the area well, and had done many patrols on his own there earlier in his career.

During the drive down to Balla Balla which was uneventful, Ncube explained what it meant. Balla means Impala, and doubled up means more Impala. It was much the same as Dousi in Shona. At Balla times two, George was in for a shock. At the junction of the road to Shabani, they stopped for a cool drink at a wayside bar. A voice came from the back of the shade, 'Hey good to see you again'. George turned and peered into the gloom. Up came a face and frame he had met at Nyamapanda.

'Whiskey Thomas' how good to see you. What are you doing down here?'

'I'm still prospecting, but now I am looking for more gold scams near Antelope Mine'

They pumped each other's hand, for a minute, then sat and reminisced for another twenty. Establishing that neither had changed in the interim years. George told briefly of his Botswana encounter, and 'Whiskey' of his 'meanderings' across the Country. Time went and Ncude appeared to remind George of an enquiry they had to do there.

A small private boarding school, set up for distant farmers and mine engineers was established at Balla Balla. There had been a complaint about some noisy dogs. It was time to look for somewhere to camp for the night also. George would ash the Head of the school for permission to find a place there, so they had water at least. The Head was agreeable and told George that the dogs in question, belonged to the Matron of the school, who was in the lad dormitory now. After chatting with the Head about the School in general, he took his leave and went to see the Matron.

Andrea, was 23 years of age. She was dive feet four inches and had the build of a hockey player. Not fat, but strong and athletic. Her face had a wide bone structure capped by light brown hair. George asked her about the dogs being noisy, which she refuted, and invited George to see himself. He agreed. In the meantime she had to check on the lads, 'Do you want to come with me" she asked, 'The kids would love visit from one of the best Police'. 'O.k. sure, where to?

Andrea led the way to the boys' dormitory, and knocked and opened the door. They walked in as the lads were running around in their pyjamas yelling and shouting. Four of the boys were on their hands and knees at the end of a row of beds. In their hands were spiders. The size of the children's hands, orange haired, baboon spiders. They were having a sort of race with them, but the spiders had no idea how to keep in a straight line. Once they left the imprisonment of the hand, they were wont to go anywhere. The children, wild with delight, were chasing and catching them after the brief escape. 'Do you want a go?' one had looked up at George and offered. 'No thanks', he politely declined.

The spiders were returned to their shoeboxes, the children to their beds. Andrea wished them a goodnight, switched off the lights, closing the door behind herself and George.

They talked amicably as they strolled across the grass lawn to Andrea's small quarters. She had to have a little dispensary, and sick bay, along with her own ling accommodation. Inviting him in, she offered supper and a bottle of wine. Gratefully accepting this, George needed the bathroom, to clean hmslef up, first.

The dogs were two 'Ridgebacks'. Tan in colour they have a particular natural line of hair, down the centre of their back. Excellent dogs for pets or protection, they were very popular dogs for families in Rhodesia. Andrea insisted he stayed the night to make sure they were not noisy. He happily accepted.

Ncude and George set off through European farmland towards the Matopos Hills. Huge fields. Each several acres of grazing land for cattle. Because of the rains, a cattle farmer had one acre per head of his stock. As the herd grazed out one paddock they were sent to another while the grass grew back again. Consequently, from the road one could see very little of interest. Ahead the hills grew prominent in the landscape, and it wasn't long before they reached the foothills, and the Rhodes Matopos National Park.

The Park was the haven for the densest population of Leopard, in Rhodesia, but they were seldom seen. Many would hunt by night, and lie up in the day. Other 'game' such a Sable Antelope, Kudu, and Impala thrived there.

On the human side, there was, at the top of a flat yellow rock, a bronze plaque commemorating the death of Cecil Rhodes, the Country's founder. He is buried Rhodesia are buried there. Previously the area had been sacred to the Kalanga people and was known as Malin. Caves in the rocks there bear ancient paintings.

In had a 360 degrees view of scintillating landscape. Huge boulders weighing tons, balanced on tiny bases, and other sat on top of each other. It was as if giant had been playing with stone and been called away, leaving them in piles and heaps.

A panoramic view showed the outcrops of rocks sticking out of rich grassy valleys. Mopane trees and scrub land gave shelter and food to animal inhabitants.

A radio message called them back to Essexvale, he was on the move again.

FIGTREE

From Essexvale to Figtree, one goes into Bulawayo, then back out from there on a different almost 90 degree angle. Essexvale was south-east, Figtree, south-west.

The road runs alongside the railway, from Bulawayo, through Figtree, and Marula, on the Plumtree. That is the Botswana border, and not exactly George's favourite place, after the sojourn in prison there. The railway line is the same that goes through Botswana via Francistown and Gaberone.

Figtree was about 40 miles out of Bulawayo, but the full tar covering, soon petered out to strip road. Two parallel lines of black top and a wide dirt shoulder on each side, for vehicle to pass. The town consisted of a Railway Station, and a single block building. In this and a Medical Centre.

Across the railway, a single Hotel stood. The road beside it, led up to the Police Camp, which was on top of a small hill, overlooking it all. White stones marked the side of the grit road up to the Camp.

The Police Camp had a Charge Office, consisting of three rooms. The single door to the Station, led immediately into the radio and general activities office. The Member in Charge's office behind it. The third room was a small armoury. In front of the Office block was a parade ground with a dirt surface.

To the right front was small bungalow, which was to be for George. Below and behind the Charge Office was another bungalow for the M.I.C. the other side of the Parade ground away from it, were houses and billets for the A.P.

The building itself was a tidy; white painted, block structure with red corrugated steel roof. Three front windows in the radio office, and a back window for the M.I.C. A well maintained low hedge was in front of the Station door, and another round to the back. A palm tree and a couple of other deciduous trees decorated the immediate surrounds. A cell block stood behind the A.P: quarters.

George had been posted here because there was just one European left. The station should have one S.O. and one P.O: but both married. The S.O: Christian Collins was there with his wife and daughter. The other had left and returned to Salisbury, where his wife came from, taking their furniture. So it was to an empty house that George moved in.

Bit by bit, he collected a bed, table and chairs and enough to keep him going. By and by, more would be added, as some of the European farmers donated a few creature comforts.

Geographically; the road and railway were still on the higer plateau of central Rhodesia. Rivers that sprang up, ran either north and into Botswana, or south to become tributaries to the Limpopo, Matopos National park was but a few miles directly south-east of Figtree.

The area of responsibility, on the southern edge, was just a few miles parallel to the road. Inside this parameter was European land. Outside was T.T.L: and the Matopos Park. This was controlled by Matopos Police Station. Cyrene was a mission Station where a road branched south and formed the boundary between the Stations.

Following the main road towards Plumtree. a small road junction at Marula was the southern limit. That road led to Kezi, which had a Police Post. From Marula, south to the Botswana border was Plumtree's between the European farmland and T.T.L: That track went north and then east to Solusi. That was the northern most point. Here a strip road led back to Bulawayo There were farm access tracks, all dirt that linked up the main road and the Solusi road. The area to cover was about 2,000 square miles.

Figtree's area had a mélange of responsibilities. Mostly European farms, who employed Africans living in their own compounds. There was an allocation of plots of land for Coloureds, (neither African nor European). These plots were 50 – 100 acres. There were Mission Stations dotted around the area, which operated Schools for the African children. There was no T.T.L. land.

George met with Christian (Chris), his wife Ann and young three year old Melissa. They found him some bedding and a pillow. Pencil was sent on shopping duty, and Chris' batman showed him around.

Chris introduced him to the A.P. which were on duty that day, and then took him to the Figtree Hotel, which was the one only 'Watering-Hole' in the town(?). The Colemans were the proprietors. Jack was a Truancy Officer in Bulawayo by morning, and ran the Hotel with his wide Pearl. She was at that time on duty as District Nurse.

To say it was a Hotel was a bit of a misnomer. The place had been registered as such, years ago, during a time when travel was by horse and wagon, to a railway station. The rooms then, could have been expected to be used. With the advent of vehicles, it rarely had overnight guests. They did occasional meal though, depending on who came in, from where.

It was a building built in the 20's. Solid foundation but mostly wood for walls and supports. It had a tiled roof. The entrance faced the Railway Station, and was one hundred yards from it. The main downstairs was now a bar it had an expansive kitchen. Jack and Pearl lived up stairs. What accommodation there was for guests was out of the back door across a ten foot walk way and a row of 'cabins' stood ready. The toilets for the bar were there also.

The first weekend George had time to have a good think about his life over the last two years. As a police man in the bush, things could not have been more different than any situation in the U.K. In T.T.L. lands, the African didn't steal much, as there wasn't much to steal. They live in kraals where, as family, everything was communal anyway. The European didn't steal from each other places like this, as they lived mile apart, and had no need to. In Dett, everyone was much the same, the only theft were perhaps of Rhodesia Railway, property, dealt with by R.R. Police.

A bit of drunkenness, and maybe a fight now and again would make good gossip amongst the European, more so at Dett than amongst farmers. The Africans may get drunk from time to time. If anything happened it rarely got to Police records unless one of them burned down the hut of another. This did happen, on occasion with the people inside it. It was hardly the dark city streets where one trod at one's own risk.

What totally different world to one he left behind. He had seen Game animals in their natural habitat, not pacing a ten by ten cage. Witnessing Hippo and crocodiles performing their own daily tasks, had been a marvel. He had visited one of the world's most spectacular Water Falls. He'd spent some time admiring the early man made engineering of Zimbabwe, and a thousand years later, Kariba. He'd handled crystals pulled straight from the ground, and watch gold being panned for.

No point in dwelling on ripping doors from huts to form a stretcher, or taking guns from a young man, in the middle of the night. They too, were new aspects of his life. A sojourn in a Botswana Prison was an experience, but he'd not like repeat that one.

His nostalgia was wiped out by a knock on the door, Andrea had arrived, without warning. She was bearing gifts of a bottle of wine, and a Chinese 'take-away' bought on her way through Bulawayo. She was as welcome as an Oasis in the Desert.

'Wow, is this how you're expected to live', she gasped.

George told her story of the bungalow's previous occupant, and with this his relocation to Salisbury.

'Things will be O.K: I have to it give some time' he assured her.

The evening and night were spent in splendid isolation. Word gets around pretty quickly at a bush station, so no one came near.

The following morning, 'Pencil' had passed by the window and re-chained how many cups of tea were required. He tactfully brought two, and retired to do some chores. Much later that morning, two head appeared into the sunlight. Andrea had to head back to Balla Balla so goodbyes were said.

'I'll come over again sometime she murmured'.

George wasn't so sure he wanted tag on his leg like this, so he verbally acquiesced and pursued it no further. Although her company was fine, he still had designs on Penny for the long term. A serious distraction may get troublesome and emotionally very messy.

George meth with his Sgt, Denderi, who was soon to be transferred to the Special Unit; Chivero and Dube. Ten constables were posted to Figtree, but they had only eight. Some of these were married and had their wives there. some had left their wives back in their T.T.L:s.

Morning duties were for George, he was the only P.O. Getting up for duty was no hardship, as the sun was up by 6.00 or 6.30, so he might as well be. The Station had one grey personnel type Land Rover, and a spare pick-up type, in green. The constables had bicycles for their patrols.

His first job was to go down to Marula to help a farmer who had a cow in trouble with a breached calf. The farmer was an old Africaaner who was slightly disabled.

The Animal Health Inspector was there, Roger Beal, so he and George left Hansie de Villiers at his cottage, and walked to the byre with a small enclosure attached. The cow was in the enclosure and sounded very unhappy. The cow's rear end. Using water and disinfectant they washed themselves up to their elbows.

Roger took out of his bag, two pieces of twine about three feet long. He told George that he was going to fed inside the cow's uterus and tie a length of twine around each of the backward facing calf's forelegs. They would then each pull gently to un-sung them and then draw the calf out. He had managed to tie the twine around each fore leg, and make its way across the nearby paddock and was maybe attracted by the taste in the air.

Totally undaunted by this interruption, Roger grabbed the snake by its tail, and flung it back into the paddock. The snake obviously felt unwanted and left. George would never have touched the thing. He was not a Rhodesian yet.

The calf was successfully delivered and the cow was much happier. So too was Hansie. George was thanked profusely for his contribution and took his leave.

Chris sent George out on first patrol the following day. This was not like Nyamapanda or Dett, where one caps where one can. Farmers were always glad to supply hospitality to the Police, so just a phone call ahead, and it was organised. Constable Moyo (1) would accompany him.

Jim Crowborough's ranch was the first port of call. The fields started at the bottom of the road to the Police Camp. His front door was a couple of miles away. Following dirt tracks George drove through vast fields with just grass growing. He stopped and admired a Brahmin bull who had the paddock to himself. Jim had Brahmin cattle and concentrated solely on these. It was a prize herd.

Reaching the house he drove up to the front, where there was a neat lawn in front, with acacias and Flame Lily bushes. The Flame Lily was the National Emblem. Jewellers would make broaches of these flowers, in fact one had been given to Queen Elizabeth, as then, Princess Elizabeth when she visited the country in 1947.

Jim was expecting him, and invited him in for a coffee, while Moyo went to chat to the staff and labourers. Moyo had been here before and knew them quite well. The house was the biggest building George had been in since the school at Balla Balla. The Reception hall was into a lounge. High walls made of stone kept it cool and panoramic windows over looked the front. Big, soft, comfy armchairs and matching settee at one end, with a rose wood, highly polished table with eight dining seats towards the other.

Jim was recently widowed, and was glad of company. Although the day to day running of the farm kept his days busy, the evenings were often a bit of a drag for him. Now there was another single man in town, they would often join together at the Figtree Hotel for a beer in the evening.

No one locally knew where Jim had got the money to buy this property. It was said that his wife had been a millionaires and had bought it some 15 years ago. Jim had been a cattle farmer in Yorkshire and knew his work well. The chance of having such a magnificent herd had been the thing of his dream. Now he had one.

George could not stay very long, he had another good way to go before reaching Jim's neighbor Tony Rosenthal, so he took his leave. Finding Moyo waiting for him was good. Moyo was one to wander away, especially when there was female staff to attend to.

Using the only routes available, which are dirt road and farm tracks, he approached the Rosenthal home. He hadn't seen much en route, because of concentrating on the road. Any oncoming vehicle had to be negotiated very carefully as there were few passing places, where the roadside scrub allowed it. Thick bushes and high grass did not permit much sight seeing either.

Tony Rosenthal was fourth generation Rhodesia. His Great Grandfather and Grandfather, had come by ox pulled wagon, and stayed right where the house stood. Tony's brother had an adjacent farm, which he would visit later. Jeanette, Tony's wife, greeted him at the door and led him inside. Tony was working and would be back later. The mornings were the essential time for these farmers. To hey the day organised and jobs allocated.

The current house had all been re-built, as the old, had been a rough place and seen better days. This one was modern, with running hot and cold water, and electricity from their own generator as well as the National Grid. They had telephones with fax machines, several vehicles for work and social use.

The farm was agricultural. Over the 2,00 Acres they had, they grew maize mostly. Regimental lines of sweet corn, all as straight as a die, a hundred yards long, and growing up to six or seven feet tall. As an alternative, there were some fruit trees, melons and vegetables. He employed thirty two Africans and sustained them and their families. The African children attended a Mission School nearby.

That evening, as George was staying over, Tony Called his brother Guy and his family over for dinner. This would save going to them and it was all wonderfully social. Tony and Jeanette had two boys Greg and Dirk. Greg was away in South Africa studying Mining. Dirk was there, he was much shorter than his father, but as strong as an ox. The Africans called him 'Little Rhino'.

Guy's wife Suzy, was a lovely bubbly woman, and they had two children. Dawn who was married and living in Bulawayo, and Clive who was at University in Salisbury.

Guy grew maize, fruit vegetables also. They explained that the original farms of the grandfather had catlle, but so many had died of various maladies that they scrapped the bovines and went into cash crops. Modern medicines could cope with so much more than in previous years, so beef and dairy herds were better protected. A lot of money had to be spent on vaccinations and veterinary services however.

The meal and company were superb. They talked late and of so many topics. They started with the rains and things relevant to local issues, broader subjects were embraced as the wine flowed, and the World put to right in general.

He was regaled with fantastic stories of their forebeaers and the pioneers of the Country. The Ox cart trek up from South Africa. Living in the wild hunting for meat with old smooth bore rifles. The first house that Grandfather built, and his father dying of malaria.

The land then was just wild savanna. Crossed by Mzilikazi's Impi when they went looking for battles. No dams, irrigation schemes, roads or other communication. Natural features of the country were taken as limits for the colonisation. Mutual agreements, honoured by handshakes, became binding in law years later. The first cattle ranches were started, but many fell to Tsetse fly and then a number of them taken, or traded with the tribesmen.

Tobacco was tried, but it grew better elsewhere. Corn was tried and it thrived on the climate and soil. Now enough of it is grown throughout Rhodesia, it feels thousands of people and is exported all over the Southern Africa Countries.

Both senior male Rosenthals were Police Reservists. These were men who could be called upon if occasion demanded to back-up the Regulars. They did undergo training from time to time so George was to see more of them in due course.

After a hearty breakfast, the patrol was resumed. The next objective was a Mission where an African school operated. Although it seemed only a gesture, it is appropriate for the Police to visit schools regularly. There is obviously a Public relations exercise involved, but also the standards they were reaching and subjects taught. A synopsis of relevant matters were required for the Political Master as well as preparing for a secondary education facility if required. Schools with a very Religious bias had a general reputation of straying into politics to far.

The Nata Mission was built by the river of the same name. Set back and in its own ground. It consisted of a school room complete with blackboard, desks and chair. A Church stood to the right of it, with an iron crucifix above the door. its gentle simplicity and unadorned austerity spoke volumes for these Missionaries. There was one man in charge, Henry Swan. He was an Englishman medium height with a full beard on his face, to compensate those receding hairs on his head. He had an African teacher. George introduced himself,

He asked the usual question of interest. How many children? How are they getting along with their studies? Is ther anything that they need, or that the Police can help with?

In answer, George learned that there was nothing they could do to help. The children are fine, and that are progressing well in class.

The patrol was to spend the evening at another Mission at Solusi, so they bade farewell and drove on. Solusi was where the tar strip road from Bulawayo, met the dirt road they were on now. There was a small township there, with a store, and a petrol station. This Mission was run by an American Evangelical Society, so what to expect was any-bodies guess.

They were welcomed by the Principal, Gilmore Peterson, who struck George as a bit self-righteous, straight away. He was then introduced to the Head of Schooling Cyril Benimore, Teachers, Beth Longbridge and Clive Rowntree. Moyo disappeared to reunite with some of the Africans, and George got his first lecture.

'We keep the body as pure as we can. No smoking no meat. We eat only fresh natural foods. We observe the Sabbath, and have prayers morning and evening. Apparently, George had been just in time to miss the evening's prayer session. At dinner, after the Blessing, they all sat down to crisps (allowed), tomatoes, avocado, and other good clean, natural food.

After dinner, table tennis game filled the time, until bedtime. George had the impression, that Ruth and Clive might be tempted to share the one bed but it would have been blasphemous to say anything. The conversation was devoid of anything controversial or Political. As neutral as Switzerland and as impotent as a Gelding. They were pretty unctuous bunch.

Both he and Moyo were glad to leave. Moyo was not allowed to smoke unless he went outside, which was unusual then. He had the same gender free desultory evening.

The journey back took them to the Homes and farms of the Barbers. Similar to the Rosenthals they had longish establishment in the Country. Not as far back or exciting as theirs, the Barbers had come out from the U.K. in the 30's and settled there. Two sons had divided their parent's farm. They each had about 200 acres, which was deemed to be a 'Plot', as opposed to a farm.

Their land had an irrigation system that provided them with Maize, vegetables, and some fruit trees. It provided sufficient profit for them to live quite well.

Fred and Janice lived alone, as their two children were away. One at University, the other worked for the District Commissioner in Fort Victoria.

Fred's brother Garry and his wife Valerie lived a mile up the road. They too had two children, who were away in the U.K. (Overseas). It was only middle of the day, and George was not to stop for dinner, but get on back to the station. A light lunch was had some home made lemonade. Also, as Police Reservists, George was to more of them.

Returning to Figtree, he promise his report for Chris the following day. He had plenty of notes but would sit and do a proper report after a shower, something eat and a beer at the Hotel.

There was something that he could not place about his bedroom. Some thing was not the same, but he couldn't place it. 'Pencil' came with his cup of tea, and broke into the wide smile.

'What is it 'Pencil' what's been happening'.

'The curtains Ishey, Your lady came back while you were gone, and put up some curtains'.

That was it. Curtains on the windows. Last time she was here, 'Pencil' had seen what was going on, so for some future privacy, the minx had come and blotted out the view from outside.

At the Charge Office, Chris was smiles and 'Nudge Nudge Wink Wink'.

'She is trying to civilise me, and I won't have it. Next time she'll bring bunches of plastic flowers and a floral tea service with sugar lumps. She should have phoned first. I could have been doing anything'. George ranted on for a few minutes, then saw the funny side of it and let up. 'She really meant well though, fair's fair. I don't think I can handle being tightened up on though, at the moment'.

'Next time she calls George, I'll send you out again, don't worry',

Sgt Dube was marching eight prisoners up the drive to the Station. His task had been to go to Bulawayo early in the morning and return by train. He was to check all the passengers on the train, and bring to the

Police Camp all those who should not have been there. A serious problem had started Africans illegally leaving the country and declaring them selves in Botswana as migrant labourers.

A labourer from Gwelo, for example, would have no reason to be here, as tribally he would be out of his area. His identification (Situpa) would show his home details. If he had work in the area he would have some sort of letter of authority to show. They could be fugitives from the law.

All these African had to be questioned as to why they were here. This was George's job, with help from the A.P: in translation. Enquiries had to be made at the last place of work and kraal. This was to be a detailed and lengthy process.

Dube was to continue this until further notice, so work was going to pile up.

Soon the cells were brimming full, and only relieved when Police vans from Bulawayo, were sent to pick up the detainees and return them from whence they came. Their first stop would be Bulawayo, where they were scrutinized again, before what ever the next process would be. George didn't much care, they were gone, and more were coming.

The full house did have its up side one night, but it was tricky while it lasted.

A call came in, that there was a bush-fire on Mr Van Heerden's farm. There was no such thing as a Fire Brigade at Figtree. The Police were the only form response that could be expected in District. So, respond they did. With no fire fighting appliances, armed with axes to cut down bushes and tree limbs. Chris and George organised the men.

Each of the A.P. was to take one of the prisoners and stay with him, as close as could be. The Camp labourers would get some sacking and join in. Chris was to transport the first wave of 'Fire Fighter' to the scene and come back for the rest.

George went with the first group.

A field of dry grass had caught fire and was spreading over a wide front. The grass was not tall but tinder dry. Van Heerden's men were already out with sacks and green branches beating the fire out and moving on. George and his men joined in.

George chopped down greenery to issue to his men. They flayed at the fire as it spread across the file. Chris' men soon joined in. A fire in such a field of grass may not mean much to a Police man, but to a farmer it is everything.

Van Heerden had cattle, and cattle need grazing. One acre per cow was required over the year, as the climate and growth rate of the grass and the cow determines. To lose a paddock this size, may mean that Van would have to rent a pasture from some one else. The fire could reach the cattle and stampede them. All kinds of scenarios added to the gravity of the night.

It was strangely picturesque with a row of flame about 100 yards long sweeping forwards, being chased by shadows of men frantically waving sacks and tree branches. It was not such a dark night, fortunately the stars provided enough to trace what was going on.

After about two hours of this, exhaustion creeping in, the wind dropped. The fire advancing on the hedge to the next paddock, stayed its progress. The defending line of silhouettes attacking the fire from behind, launched another assault. Ordered on by Chris, they smothered the flames. A further twenty minutes to walk the length of the sooty line, to make sure, Van was a bit happier.

His thanks were short. It was important to get back and make sure all the heads were accounted for. Missing prisoners were definitely no on the agenda. To the relief of Chris and George all were safely back in the fold. Extra rations to what they had been doing. The A.P. 'holding the fort' at the station would not be troubled, but for George, the radio schedule had still to be kept at 07.00.

Even Member in Charge's such Stations, had to go out on Patrols. Radios had come in from Bulawayo speaking of concern that African villains were fleeing to the T.T.L.s. Chris had to go and see the Coloureds that had plots in our areas, adjacent to the T.T.L: belonging to Nyamandhlovu, north of us. He would be away for one night, but do a road patrol during that night stopping vehicles leaving Bulawayo.

As Chris took to the road, he was leaving George in Charge. He had enough to do with the supply of 'Runners' that Sgt Dube brought in, on top of everything else. He was sure he could cope, he had to. His only hope was that nothing major took place to add to his load. He knew his prayers went unheard, when a serious call came in. it came from the farm of Nigel Lester of 'Klipspringer' farm near Cyrene. It came on the afternoon of Chris' second day out.

The fast train coming up from Plumtree, had run into the back of the slow train, going in the same direction.

A million questions formed in George's mind as he gathered a team of all the of duty A.P. he could lay his hands on. He piled all the medical equipment he could find into the spare Land Rover. No point in delaying things, he told the on-duty African Constable in the Charge Office to call Bulawayo for help straight away. He wanted Ambulances and assistance there,pronto.

'Also radio to Chris and get him back there directly as soon as he could.'

The farm was a short fifteen minute drive away, he did it ten. To his enormous relief, there had been no derailment. The trains stood there with one locomotive crunched into the rear guards van of the other. Fortunately the open country had enabled the driver to see far enough ahead and apply the braked.

His actions reducing damage to a minimum. There were a lot of shaken up bodies inside though.

The first to attend to was personal injuries. The fast up was O.K. the guards had been through them. The 'slow' up had taken the brunt of the shunt.

Working his way through the train, there was nothing more than a sprained wrist, when standing passengers had been thrown from their feet. Passing up the length of the carriages and immediate attention to those who had sustained minor bumps and bruises. A party of children had been visiting Plumtree under the supervision of local Lions Club.

The attendant Lions Members were glad that their 'charges' were uninjured.

The work to clear the mess up, was not a job for the Police, but the Rhodesia Railways. A report would still have to be field. To George's great relief along came Chris, who, as M.I.C. would said report. Another check along the carriages for any broken bones, or damaged property in case of future claim, was conducted.

It was still a mystery, why the signals hadn't slowed the 'fast up'? Why had the railways station at Marula not realized what would happen? These questions were not the domain of George, nor Chris, but they had to be asked. A serious accident enquiry would be undertaken, so the two of them had to collate as much detail as possible.

George had names; times; injuries; and visual damage recorded. Chris took statements from Drivers, Guards, and coalmen/stokers. Sgt Dube had been instructed by George to try and trace any witnesses not on the trains. Most of the bases were covered as far as possible.

Chris took George to one side. 'Have I got story for you' he said

'Come on what is it'.

'Wait until we are back at the station'.

'Well come on, what is it?'

'What's what?'

'This big deal story you have for me'.

'Well. You remember the sanctimonious Director of the Selusi Mission, who kept his body Holy and doesn't smoke, eat meat or tell lies'.

'Yeah sure'.

'Last night on the road bloke I stopped him and this other guy, Cyril something. They pulled up, and the inside of the car smelled awful. They had been stuffing their faces with 'Finger licking good' chicken and chips,

'Did you check the ashtrays?'

'No, I didn't see any 'bird' either, but what a pair of hypocrites they turned out to be '.

'I bet they were out for the evening enjoying themselves, while the other two were rolling each others bones as well'.

George had another Patrol go on not too long after that. This time, again up near the Barbers, but he had to walk 'Green routes'. There had been a growing tendency for groups of armed burglars attacking outlying farms. The farms that had been attacked were not far off a road, and close enough for vehicular get away. Most farmers had guns would be ready to use them to protect themselves, family and farm. Orders are orders, and evacuation routes had to be planned for such farms.

Gary and Valerie were happy to see George again, and he explained the reason for the visit. Gary explained the layout of the farm and walked him around.

'You have to see this while you are here' said Gary.

'What is it?'

'Come on inside this cave'.

Breathtaking scenes painted by bushmen decorated the walls. Paitings the also adorned the caves in the Matopos National Park, that he hadn't yet seen.

Drawings by Africans long since disappeared from there, maybe banished by the Impis of Mazilikazi, or even long before that. George wondered if the tribesmen he may have seen on that ill fated Patrol of the Kalahari were descendants of the people who painted these pictures on the walls.

Pictures of hunting game and men with spears chasing a bleeding antelope.

Colours, still picked out the markings on their bodies, and the splashed of blood that were natural to a hunt with spears. An incredible experience, seeing ages old African Art.

A few days after finishing these escape routes, George was at the Figtree Hotel for a beer, but was decidedly unwell. He could not handle a glass, he was feverish, temperature, definitely unwell.

Transport was called for, and George was off to hospital in Bulawayo.

The hospital was called Mpilo, which is Ndebele means 'Life'. He was taken to bed and test tubes of blood, taken from him, though he barely knew it.

The first two days were a blurr, through perpiration and sleep. At least he was coherent enough to talk to a Doctor (Not a witch one). To his great relief, he was diagnosed as having 'Tick' fever. He had been a bit lax on his camoquins of late, so that he had not got malaria was in a way a blessing. Not since Morosi Dam had he encountered serious mosquitoes, but there was always a chance.

There were three types of 'Tick' that were prevalent at the time. They were all parasites. The 'Blue' tick usually clung to the ears of dogs and cattle (sheep were rare there). They did not cling to humans. They were eliminated by running the animals through 'Dips' that were like elongated mechanics inspection pits. Filled with water and a detergent, specially for 'ticks' and lice, dogs and cattle ran the gauntlet.

The brown tick clung onto humans but one just pulled them off, or burned them with a cigarette end. The 'Ban Tick' was the bugger of them all. They would look like a brown tick. To George who was covered in freckled, it was another brown spot. If the tick moved or caused irritation, one swept if off or used finger nail to dislodge it. Obviously George had tried to remove a supposed brown tick with his finger nail, it being a Ban tick left its head in George's leg.

Tick fever, very much like malaria, resulted in a fever, and all the sign symptoms that George had shown. The good thing was that after treatment, it was not a recurring nightmare that malaria could be. Neither was it Chargeable in the B.S.A. Police.

George spend a week in Mpilo, but after four days, he was ready to go. He could walk about, chat with the other people in his ward, and felt fine. He had a visiting Doctor, with an entourage of inters, look at his legs and display his case history notes that George had played a lot of sports. Hence the musculature of his thighs and calves.

He was bored and wanted out. Eventually he was signed of, and picked up, by Valerie Barber. She took him home, to Figtree. He always had a 'crush' on her since then.

The news that awaited him was good. His application for leave had been approved, and that next Sunday, nearly all the European in the area were off for a cricket match.

In his absence, a not worried, but bothered group of the populace had come up with idea of a welcoming party. Being as distance, venue etc were difficult, a neutral venue had been sought. A team from Figtree, were to play team from Plumtree at Marula.

A Marula, is a fruit, common to very few places. It is like a large Lichee which one gets as deset at Chinese restaurant. It is white and fleshy, around a pip or stone in the centre. Films have been made of drunken elephants, giraffes and monkeys who have eaten the fallen fruits of Marula. Its fruit falls when ripe, and starts to deteriorate. When eaten by an animal, it ferments in the stomach and causes the animal to be intoxicated. Now it is made into a liqueur for humans too, so they can fall about after a few.

The stage was set at the Marula School. A test match of the lowest order between those representing the Powers of Law and Order from Figtree, and the Noble Denfenders of our National Borders at B.S.A. Police Plumtree. Picnic baskets abounded, a Braai vleis arranged and meat brought. Salads and deserts made by the ladies of both sides. Whites and gear had been scrabbled together by all and sundry. Someone had a bat here, another had some stumps in his garage, it all came together. George met up with the Member in Charge who had welcomed him back from the Botswana prison, who was still at Plumtree. A festive atmosphere prevailed.

For Figtree, there was Chris and George from the Police, two Barber brother, two Rosenthal brother and one son, Dirk 'the Little Rhino'. Jim Crowborough and Nigel Liston made up nine. Then Roger the A.H.I. made ten, and Van Heerden made full complement. The Plumtree team was similarly made up. They had more E.P. than us, but Customs and Immigration there, added a couple, and some ringers from another station made eleven.

Because of time, duties and distance, for every body, the game way limited to thirty 'overs' each side, with lunch at the break. Plumtree won the toss and went in to bat. George kept wicket for Figtree. Few of either team had done any sport for some years. The mobility factor played a large part in the score, as Figtree's players were on average some twenty years older than Plumtree's young P.O:s. They being the same age as Tony's son Dirk.

At lunch, everyone are heartily and could not bat after, as a result. Plumtree won the day. After Chris had batted he was called away, back to work, but he hadn't scored many anyways. A very sociable way to get to know ones neighbours. It was to be significant for George to meet again with Plumtree Oficcers, and also with some of their reservists.

Jim brought George back to Figtree, to find Chris had been called to a traffic accident. How anyone can hit another on a strip tar road suggested drunkenness, but on return, it had been two African drivers each forgot their left from their right. (Maybe one had slipped from the net at Dett). What was of greater concern was that a boomslung snake had entered Chris' bungalow.

Above George's bungalow, at the top of the rise, was a water storage enclosure. It was up there so it would provide a bit of pressure for the buildings below. Where there is water, there lives frogs. Where there are frogs, snakes.

Ann was beside herself with worry about Melissa, so they leapt into action. Having seen it done before,

George grabbed a mop and approached the defending creature. The boomslung is a black fanged snake. It doesn't spit, and it has to get its bite in the back of its mouth in order to inject poison. Offering the open door, against a mop, the snake chose the path of discretion, and left the building.

One Sunday, Chris, Ann, Melissa and George had been invited to 'Klipspringer' by Nigel and his wife. They were to play a little tennis, have a bar-be-que, a nice day out. He had named his farm after a little antelope no bigger than a terrier dog, with antlers about the size of an adults fingers. He had a curious story to tell.

His ranch was geographically the closest cattle herd to the Matopos. He had five hundred 'Hereford' cows, with a bull. This is what he told George.

'Three weeks ago, the cows were in that south paddock. They had just been put in that one, for fresh grazing. They are all day, as they do, and in the morning I noticed they had moved to the far side of the field.'

'At first I thought nothing of it, but little by little, I realized that they were losing 'condition' not gaining it. For the life of me, I couldn't think why, so I called Roger the A.H. who came down and checked them out for me. He was stumped as well. He took grass samples and water samples. A week later he telephoned to say that nothing was wrong in the samples.'

Walking around the paddock, trying to fathom out what was wrong, I came across some leopard spoor. There were tracks all around the field, but I wasn't missing any of the cows. The leopard's prints circled the paddock, but nothing was taken.'

'I called the Game Rangers in the Matopos and told them. They sent a guy out to have a look. He guessed that the leopard was playing with the herd. The cows were eating all day, and looking at the cows hoof prints, the leopard is getting upwind of them. The smell of him would frighten the cattle across the field. So, instead of resting all night, the cows are running around the paddock. He's having a laugh.'

Nigel and the Ranger set a trap, which the leopard did not fall for, but he took one of the calves.

A week later, he was back. The cows had been running around all night. Even a change of paddock did not help, because a hunting leopard is not going to be fooled by that.

Various traps and baits were laid. The Ranger had to be careful, because he had to have a legitimate reason to kill a leopard.

The cat never returned after that. He hadn't returned or taken a calf, he hadn't given them the run around he'd gone.

Neither the Ranger nor his colleagues had ever heard of that before, a predator, such as a leopard, fooling about with a herd of cattle.

'That's quite a story' said Chris, 'Do you think it will last?'

'No idea, just hope so'.

The system was that each serving member of the Force, were entitled to so many days off per year. That could be accrued so that (before the age of flights) one could sail back to the U.K. for a holiday. The accruement of leave still stood. George had taken no leave for just over two years, and was thus able to take a long break.

He had been planning, and with the assistance of a Travel Agent in Bulawayo, his time was due.

I was a fond farewell, as George was off the next weekend. He didn't know it then, but he would be back.

HOLIDAY.

George had been liaising with a Travel Agent in Bulawayo for a holiday package, for him to take all of his accrued leave and do as much as he could with it. The lady at the Agents had come up with this.

Train from Bulawayo to Cape Town. 1 week stay.

Coach Tour from Cape Town to Durban 5 nights, along the 'Garden Route', which is the Indian Ocean side of South Africa.

Two days in Durban

Cruise from Durban via the Seychelles and Mauritius and return to Durban.

Coach Tour from Durban to Johannesburg via Switzerland and Kruger National Park

Four days in Johannesburg then return to Bulawayo by Air.

The first leg of this journey was the now familiar railway line from Bulawayo. It was the fast train so could not board at Figtree. It was strange to pass through it though. same He track had he crossed had ministered mildly injured passengers. He had crossed and re crossed it thousand times.

He had a sleeping berth and a compartment or less to himself He had a good book to read, he fine. Passing through Plumtree there was passport check at the border. He was on his British passport, and just hoped that the Immigration on the Botswana side, had forgotten his previous visit.

On through to Francistown, few off and a few on, the locomotive picked up some speed and on he went. Same un-interesting landscape as before. Had it grown? Was there more houses now, than before. A lot can happen in a year. It had been about that long. He could still remember the lament Sabuseeling

Rattling Clickety-clicking, on went the train through Malape and Mahalape next stop Gaberone. The National Capital where he had been questioned about being in the Country without having done the proper process of entry. His good name, now without blemish, as appeals had been made and accepted. He was no International gun-runner any more.

Sleep claimed much of the rest of the journey missed Kimberly and the Karoo, and read outskirt of Cape Town enclosed the railway lines.

Here in the Cape, he would look up and stay with John Piper, who had finished his 'three. with the found word here in C.T.

Over the next few days he had a terrific time, exploring the City, while John had to work. He hired a car and drove out to Stellenbosch, where the Cape's Viticulturists produce their rich, fruity wines. XXQ1ite wine was never George's favourite but he tried them anyway. The red wines were so good. He was no expert at telling a Sauvignon for a Cabernet, but such tasty fare could not possibly be ignored. Back in Cape Town he saw Groot Schur hospital, where Dr. Christain Barnard had developed his heart transplant surgery.

One day was devoted to Table Mountain. He was not too fond of cable Cars but he had to try it. He was not going to pass on chances to do new things. The ride was a bit of a heart racer. Table Mountain can be climbed from the land side by road or foot. The Cable Car was up the face of the sheer cliff. Looking down it was a hell of [a] fall if anything went wrong. The summit was as it was called a table top. The view was incredible. To the south and 180 degrees was the sea. He hadn't seen any sea for three years. Not far below and to the east, was where the warm Indian Ocean, met the cooler South Atlantic. Land wards, the coastal towns, he did not know but the bare, open land, stretching north to where he had come.

He bought books on the history of the Cape, and its City. Dutch Settlers, Huguenots, fleeing from pogroms in the 17th Century. They came and traded, settled and prospered. It was the major sea route from Europe to the East Indies, until the British wanted it.

Notwithstanding the British Colonial history, Cape Town still had Newlands. One of the sacred hearts of Rugby. As Twickenham is to English Rugby, Newlands onc of such homes to South African A Saturday was spent watching rugby, as the whole day is devoted to games. Early games on the hallowed turf would be for youngsters, getting older groups after. These were 'Curtain Raisers' for the big matches.

The Coach trip was a South African Railways bus. It seemed odd, but then a Travel Company is for all kinds of travel. The coach was new, with air conditioning and had seats for thirty. Only a dozen were occupied. The driver was a short, tubby man, very chatty and friendly. George sat near the front, just behind him. He offered his name as Bob, nothing else.

The others on the bus were a couple of twenty or so year olds who were obviously a pair of lovers or newly weds There was a family of five consisting of Mamma Bear; Pappa Bear ; two boys of about 13 and 12 respectively and a daughter of about 10. They looked like South Africans, and spoke to each other in Africaans. A

Family of three, Ma and Pa and a daughter of about 14, who also spoke to each other in Africaans. The three that seem an enigma to George, were a mother, father and daughter from New Zealand. The daughter had short brown hair and brown eyes. She was in George's age range. She attractive, but looked a little out of place there.

The first stop was at an ostrich farm. They trooped off the bus in crocodile fashion, like all good coach tourists do. Waiting for the Guide to assemble and address them, they looked around taking in the new sights and sounds.

The guide dispensed his absolute knowledge about Ostriches and gave opportunity for humour when comparing the female, and male of the species. The female had dull brownish grey plumage, whereas the male, whose outrageous black and white feathering was more sought after.

Ostriches have at one time, lived virtually all over the Continent of Africa. They were considered by the Egyptians as creatures of authority and nobility. They feature on Bushman paintings. Fossils and skeletal remains indicate that these non-flying birds have been on earth for 120 million years. They do NOT put their heads in the sand.

Apparently nothing of the Ostrich goes to waste, ᵉxcept the eyes. Even the beak and claws are used. These are cut and highly polished for necklaces and ornaments. The plumage is exported all over the World.

Here at Oodtshoon there have been Ostrich farms, since 1891 when it was mainly the feathers that were Commercially used. The skin is tanned now, and is a very good quality leather. The meat is packed and frozen and also exported allover the World.

The lecture over, they filed out to a waiting enclosure The guide picked out George for a demonstration of the strength of an Ostrich egg. George was quite a big lad just under six feet and weighing thirteen stones (80 kilos). He was a bit doubtful that he should stand on one of the eggs. Being reassured that all would be well; first one foot, then with a helping hand, the other, he was standing on an egg.

Two small Africans, one in blue silks, the other in red, mounted a couple of saddled ostriches. They rode over to a fence that circled a pool, which had a circumference of about 100 metres. 'Ready, Steady Go' shouted the guide. The pair chased each other round for three laps, the blue being the winner by about 4 lengths.

'So, as you see, a lot of things can be done with Ostriches' concluded the guide. The program over, the tourists went to lunch there, eating an Ostrich meat and egg omelette. George thought that was an interesting morning. The afternoon was to be so also.

The Kango caves were part of a limestone ridge parallel to the Swartberg mountain range. Modern man discovered them in the 17th Century. Later explorations of the 16 miles or so of the caves, and the discovery of tools and strange drawings, reveal that man sheltered in the caves 80,000 years ago.

With organised lighting, the stalactites and stalagmites gave some wonderful images. Where the two meet there was mental opportunity to visualise a Madonna and Child, a frozen waterfall another.

The night was spent at an Hotel in the town. George chatted to the Johnson members of the party. He discovered that Beth, the daughter was getting over a rather messy separation from a previous arrangement with a chap. She was accompanying her parents on a newly retired tour, before settling down to serious stagnation.

She was perfectly happy to talk with George, and they struck up a very congenial relationship. She had a degree in physics, and was between jobs

The second day of the tour was mostly all sitting and riding, admiring the views. They stopped at a single span bridge, which has over a jet black river. The river was called the Kaaimans River. It was black because of the minerals that it had absorbed coming down from the Drakensberg Mountains, inland. This range of mountains followed the coast, some miles inland from south-west to north-east for 600 miles (1,000 klms). They were then in the eastern Cape Province near the towns of George and Knysna. The panoramic views of the mountains to one side and the sea to the other was spell binding.

The Hotel that night, was The Beacon Island Hotel, at Plettenburg Bay. George sat with the trio from Palmeston, New Zealand. They were having a 'big travel' having just retired from farming. Talk was of Rugby and Cricket. The lady had a row of pills in front of her, and she explained that were for various ailments. George said he would always remember her as 'The oldest Hippie in Plettenburg Bay'. He was invited to visit them, he made it to Kiwi Country.

The Hotel was built on an isthmus. sea splashed around three sides of the hotel. No one could leave down on the rocks, it was glassed in. It made a terrific natural display. George, by virtue of her parents going to bed, managed to persuade Beth to stay behind and 'tarry' some with him. She did. She was excellent company and the two got along together really well. They agreed to accompany each other on the rest of the journey

On day three, was mostly driving up the coast, still more easterly than north. The target was Port Elizabeth.

The history of the City of Port Elizabeth, was o more modern than ancient. The really old part of that was unwritten by the early tribes that dwelt there. It is believed that Vasco Da Gama and Bortolomeu Dias had stopped there for fresh water in the late 15th Century. The first recorded details come from the Dutch east India Company in 1652, who used it as a port. They then had problems with the British from the Cape who wanted to take it over.

In 1799 the British built a fortress to repel any invading Napoleonic Frenchmen. During the 2nd Boer War a Concentration Camp was established. To commemorate this War, a statue was erected remembering the horses and mules that died. Interesting philosophy that. A memorial to the horses, and forget the concentration camp.

The name of the City did not stem from anything Regal, but Elizabeth was the name of a Cape Colonys Governor Sir Rufane Donkin. Records tell of battle against the nearby Xhosa tribe since 1820.

It was still a major sea port and quite industrialised. A few tankers and grain carriers could be seen. A rail link to Cape Town, and another to the interior Cities of Kimberley and Bloemfontein kept the Port busy. Beth and George marvelled at the history of the town. They soon had a rapport which was mutually enriching.

On the road the following day, rich rolling grassland and farms filled the scenery to the land, while the sea continued to dominate the east. It was less than 200 miles from Port Elizabeth to East London, which was their next destination. Beth sat next to George on the bus, and their mutual admiration of each other and the view, seemed to have the approval of the senior Johnsons. It turned out to be a fairly short day on the road because of this.

Now in the Eastern Cape Province, East London had a similar history as P.E. It was first used as a port on the banks of the Buffalo River, which remains the focal point of the harbour. The early settlement became a supply depot for the British troops engaged in battles against the Africans and the Boers since 1800. Two areas of Tribal Homeland, the Ciskei and the Transkei, were just a few miles outside the City limits.

In 1935 a Double-Decker bridge was built here, it was the only one of its kind in Southern Africa and linked parts of the city, divided by the Buffalo estuary. It Was an interesting feature of the dock-lands.

The foothills were getting closer to the shoreline, when they turned up inland. This day was to be spent in Lesotho. Not just a home land almost a Country within a Country. It was land that Xhosa had occupied for untold years. The history books tell of two tribes, the Thembo and the Pondo. They orinated in Central Africa and migrated here. They settled, each tribe talking different banks of the Mtata river. They occasionally had fights but it seems they eventually formed the Xhosa tribe, and their Capital was Umtata. That was in the late 1870's

The area later became the recruiting ground for the Witwatersand, The gold mines at Johannesburg. In 1980, a Town Hall was built in neo classical design, from local sandstone.

The driver parked the coach and left them in the hands of a tour guide. The African guide took them to a mock up of an African village. The residents had dressed in their finest beads and grass skirts for a celebration dance. George had spent more hours than he could remember walking to and from and into African villages, so he knew a fake when he saw one. There was a tourist gimmick which was a bit 'tacky'. Small African boys were begging for money. Big smiles and upturned palms, as the visitors passed by.

George had wandered off a little way. Beth and her parents were enthralled by the new surroundings He was going back to chat with the driver of the coach Bob. He was approached by an upturned palm, behind which was a very astonished boy, who was told in his own language, that no money would be forthcoming. Ndabele was a sister language from the Zulu and Xhosa.

Having used up rolls of film, the group reformed at the bus and continued the tour. The road from

Umtata to the coast, was a good road, but twisted and turned following the contours, and then a river. Beth's enthusiasm that George decided that his cynicism be left un-uttered, so he kept his mouth shut.

A few miles from Umtata, the driver spoke on the coach's P.A. system, that up ahead was a tall rock face, high above the river that they were following. This he told hem was where the Great Chief Chaka of the Zulus threw off the top, those who he wished to punish. The sins of the punished are not recorded, but could have been for anything from cowardice, to his own displeasure.

At the foot off the pass, the river Umzimvubu estuary, emptied into the warm Indian Ocean. There were hills guarding the river mouth and a beach to its right. Dense forest covered the hills and surrounding land. A small town nestled under the trees by the beach. It was somewhat reminiscent of a Cornish or Devonian seaside retreat.

In 1845, the Pondo King, Kaku, had set up his base here. In 1878 he invited the English to make the area part of the Cape Colony. Two British Representatives had arrived and raised the Union Flag.

It is not clear why the town was named Port St, John. It had been known as a wild coast. When the Indian Ocean raged, many ships had gone down in these waters. The inlet had been used for smuggling as well as a refuge and water point for coastal sailors. Not far up the coast were mangrove swamps and dense forestry.

This was the last night of the tour. The next day was Durban and for most of the party, back home. For George it was Durban, and then a Cruise, and of course farewell to Beth.

The drive out of Port St John backtracked the route in the road wove its way back to Umtata, then turned right to Durban. The scenery was still impressive, and the trees diminished in the rolling grassy hills, of Natal. It was called 'The Valley of a thousand hills'. From the uplands of Umtata the way dropped gradually to the coast. The route along the coast, was a procession of seaside towns and resorts. Then they arrived, at the main bus and coach depot of Durban.

The Travel Agent had found George an Hotel. It was just one street back from the main beach front.

His first full day was spent having a long walk around. After sitting in a coach every day, over the last week, strolling round the City was a way to stretch his legs again.

The State of Natal was named by Vasco de Gama in 1497, after Portuguese word from Christmas. It was KwaZulu to the Africans. Port Natal was the unimaginative named for the Port of Natal. It was renamed after Sir Benjamin D'Urban a Cape Governor in 1835.

The discovery of Gold in the Witwatersand and the construction of a major rail link between Johannedburg and the Coast at Durban had changed the town into a major Port. The shoreline of sandy beaches and bathing facilities created a playground for holidaymakers from all over South Africa.

Durban was also a melting pot of races. Apart from the obvious Africans, Boers and British, the coast had become a citadel for Asians. Although in those years, the Asians had settled, they had their own Community, apart from the other. Many had created their own business, favouring jewellery, and imports from the East.

It was the first time the George had seen Richshaws being pulled around the streets as a form of transport. The ment the pulled them, had brilliant costumes that they would wear on special occasion, but not for daily work.

George checked with a shipping agent, the details of his cruise. He hated to leave things until the last minute, then find he hadn't time

'The Father's Moustache' was a local bar, recommended by the Hotel reception. After dinner at the Hotel, George wandered to the sea front boulevard to find it. A mélange of people were wrapped around the bar, and he distinctly heard English being spoken by an Englishman.

He introduced himself to a chap called Billy Johnson, whose stage name was 'Trente Morgan'. Billy had a contract to be part of the entertainment on the very cruise that George was on. Billy was from Bradford. He was a signer who told jokes and stories. He stood five feet eleven and had light brown hair, in the image of Elvis Presley, but a bit longer at the back.

Quite a serendipitous meeting indeed. George already knew some one on board. He had the self-confidence to meet new people, and on the other hand, was not afraid to be on his own. Ot have an on-going acquaintance was indeed a bonus. He bought some beers and the two got to know each other better.

The pub had live music later that evening. A group consisting of a bass player, a drummer, and a guitarist, led by a pianist. The vocals were joined in by all, and the pianist was the leader/spokesmen as well. The atmosphere was friendly and fun. It was a thoroughly good night, and fortunately ended in the right bed in the right Hotel.

The following evening was a repeat of the last, with the added bonus of meeting another of the entertainers, Jean Galloway, billed as Rae Shears, was a petite, auburn haired lady. Also a singer and entertainer she had a bubbly personality and was in a good shape, with a pretty face. Jean stood about five feet tall, only, and weighed about eight stone.

THE CRUISE.

George took a car from the Hotel to the Docks. He left and would be returning for a night at the end of the voyage. He wore his light blue safari suit, with knee length light blue socks, and his Game skin shoes.

The S.S. Oceanic Independence was quite a fine looking Cruise Liner. Not as big as ships like the Q.E.2, but impressive. Block lower hull, with white superstructure, and a couple of red chevrons on the funnels.

Embarkation was rather disorganized, with hundreds of people, trying to be orderly, but wanting to be first. Gangways separated various groups of ticket holders, like going to a Sports Stadium. At the top of each ramp, lists showed who was berthed where. George's cabin was U 169 which sounded more like a German Submarine. It was not first class, but had a 'window'. At least he wouldn't have to stoke the boilers if there was trouble, it accommodated two, and he was to share until the Seychelles where after he would be alone.

Hector McGuire was his cabin 'mate'. He was six feet one inch tall, long brown neck length hair and a moustache. He was a likeable easy going chap from Cape Town. Like many other passengers he was on a break from University there. This was a good Omen for George, because he accepted immediate introduction to many fellow travelers. He was neat and clean had excellent manners, and was from wealthy parents. So too were many of the students on board.

At sailing time, the decks were filled with well wishers and families, throwing streamers to each other, from deck to shore. Blowing kisses and waving, as though they were going off to some far and distant place, never to be seen again. George knew nobody on the shore, so he made space for some one who did.

Different cabins and decks had separate dining facilities. George and Hector were to share a table at their respective galley. A retired couple Harry and Sybil Braithewaite were to share the same table. It was a table for six, but only four allocations. Dinner was not formal, but one had to be 'smart', no jock-strap and trainers allowed. The breakfast and lunch were less dressy.

The crew were all Asians, but the Senior Officers, European. The waiters looked after the tables very efficiently and the food excellent. In fact one could virtually eat the clock around. Apart from the normal three times a day meal schedules. At midnight, a buffet was available, and that too was superb.

The Cruise was to have two stops, one at Mauritius another at the Seychelles. However the short sojourn at Mauritius was to be cancelled. A reason was given over the tannoy but no one seemed to understand the P.A. system a later consensus of opinion was that there was internal trouble there. The Island was under Portuguese rule, but they had an Independence struggle going on. In order to avoid any trouble for the passengers, the decision to by pass it was taken. This now meant several days of non-stop sea views. The hot tropical sun, and the reflecting sea, meant burning.

This didn't sit very well with George. Although he had met a few other people, being fair skinned, he was not inclined to lie in the sun. as one young lady put it, 'You'll go like a prawn'. He found shade in various lounges, and read quite a lot. He also explored the ship thoroughly and often poked his nose into places that it shouldn't have been. There was no trouble, just a quick apology and gone.

Evenings were different. After dinner the ships entertainment came to life. Billy and Jean (Trente and Rae) alternated shows, as well as other acts, dancing troupes. The passengers were to join in, on some nights as well.

Turn about night was coming up, where the men dressed as women, and vice versa. This is when Hectors friends all helped out.

Billy (Trente) had all kinds of his stage clothing, including a wig. He had been chatting up Dawn, so they got themselves arranged, in their own privacy. Jean (Rae) was doing the cabaret that night, so at first she didn't join in. Four other girls of Hectors group helped him out with a button up dress in a mid blue colour, which didn't quite cover the hairs on his chest and had to help shut with a bootlace at the top.

A rather reluctant George was eventually attired, with floral wrap around skirt, and a black halter neck top. finished off with some beads and a headscarf. Hector lent Michelle a jacket, and from somewhere she managed to get a bowler hat. She was O.K. for shorts.

The dressing up was to be judged as a competition, by the First Officer, in his uniform (he wasn't going to win), the Director of Entertainment, and Jean (Rae).

As each person arrived at the back-stage area, they were given a number, and were to parade in front of the judges in order.

George's femininity was lost with his broad shoulders and legs that could kick-start a Jumbo Jet. Still, with winging his beads, and a pair of underpants showing rom his borrowed handbag, he went down well with the audience.

Every contestant drew laughs from the crowd, but the inner Was a small chap who had dressed up as though he was pregnant, and pulled faces like Les Dawson.

They stayed thus dressed for the rest of the evening, except the winner who had to give birth, before enjoying the acts. After she had done her performance, Jean dressed up as a little boy with a cap, a sort of Jimmy Clitheroe. While the music continued, courtesy of the resident orchestra, An enormous South African man wanted to dance with her.

The Africaaner stood six feet six inches and had huge shoulders. He was a burly man and must have weighed nearly 300lbs. He had his little brother with him, who was only an inch shorter. He was a giant too. The Africaaner, picked up Jean and put her sitting on his forearm. Her head was just a shade above his, as he waltzed her around, like a child, to everybody's amusement.

The ship docked at Victoria, on the Island of Mahe This Island is the largest of the enormous archipelago, which makes up the Republic of Seychelles. This Island is 28 kilometres long and 8 wide. The Capital, Victoria, is reputed to be one of the smallest Capitals in the World. It had been visited by Vasco da Garna, and had been the subject of a 'Tug of War' between France and Britain. In 1812 the Union Flag was hoisted and had remained.

Hector was disembarking here to stay for a while. They shook hands and wished each other well. George had the cabin to himself now.

Coaches had been arranged to take passengers to various places of interest, on the Island. In Victoria, there were markets full of locally made products, and a new Cathedral. The coaches were doing circular trips, so a short time later, George found himself with Billy at a beautiful resort called Beau Vallon. It was the essence of a tropical island beach. The sands were white and smooth. Behind the sands, palm trees shaded the edge of the beach. Finding a coconut, the two of them in swimsuits ran along the beach, passing the coconut between them like a rugby ball. There was no chance of kicking it in bare feet.

Along the beach, some locals were pulling in a fishing net. The fishermen had gone out in their long boat, laid the net, and were hauling it back. The boat looked as though it had been fashioned from one huge tree, and been hacked hollow. While one end of the net had remained on shore, or brought in by the boat, the other needed muscle.

Billy and George set about helping with the catch. It took a lot of heaving and grunting to land the net, and to them, it didn't seem much to show for the work. The locals however were very grateful for the help, and showed it, by offering the two some warm food. This food was a breadfruit, cooked over an open fire.

The outer case was to be discarded, but the thick inside was quite tasty. Its consistency was doughy, hence perhaps the title, breadfruit. They bade farewell to the fishermen and made their way back to the ship.

The next day, on shore, George wanted to swim in a lagoon. He found one with a coral reef protecting the inner waters. It was a scene so picturesque that a postcard could be made from it. In the lagoon, was moored a sailing yacht, so obviously the coral did not completely lock the waters in. George swam out to the boat. The water was so clear, he dipped his head under water and could watch fish gliding around beneath him. The sea was warm, not like a bath, but just above cool, so that being in it, was so comforting and pleasant.

In order not to offend, he made it to the yacht and turned and went back. Nobody appeared to be on board but it was easier to avoid trouble than court it. He laid on the beach in the shade and read his book, before going back to the Cruise ship. All passengers had to be back for midday. The ladies had been shopping and had sun hats and hand woven things, that caught their eye.

Due to sail that night, no further exploration was permitted. The crew had to count heads to make sure that all were that should be there. They were on their way back to Durban.

The journey back had only one special evening, and that was George's invite to dine with the captain. This invite although with some merit, was a formality for those with cabins named after 'U' boats.

In fact, it wasn't the Captain that joined the table, it Was his First Officer. It was strange trying to engage the whole table in conversation at first. Harry and Sybil had up most of their chat on George when Hector was there. He sold Insurance, and she was a housewife, man so the First Officer became the target of questions. The man was obliging and told of his days at sea, but it wasn't exactly 'Moby Dick' stuff.

In fact it came to George, to regale them with some stories of his time in Rhodesia, that lit the table conversationally. He wasn't Rudyard Kipling, but he had done something in his life, which few others had done.

The rest of the voyage was plain sailing. Just that, plain sailing. Those that wanted to go from vanilla skin to coffee coloured, did it. He did not want to go from milky to prawny, and then be sore for days. Despite modern creams and lotions, he stayed out of the sun most of the time. Durban appeared back on the horizon, as it got nearer he realised that this leg of the holiday was at an end.

Goodbyes to the girls and to Billy and Jean were said. He was on his own again.

The following day they exchanged details back in Durban, he stayed for the night he had before resuming his tour of South Africa on the next leg. This was another coach journey ending in Johannesburg. It was spent having a few beers at the 'The Fathers Moustache' and it was there that he met Maxine. Maxine was a native of Johannesburg, just up for weekend. She hadn't found anywhere to stay, but as George had an Hotel room the problem ceased to exist. They exchanged details, and Maxine promised to look him up, in a week or so's time when he arrived in Jo'Berg..

At the bus station he found his driver and fellow travellers, packed his holdall in the trunk and found a seat.

The others on the coach, were four lady nuns, a family of four Africaaners, two pairs of middle aged couples; and two young men in company. The driver's name was Tim. He was an escapee from London Transport, making a new life for himself, in the sun. Tim was a small wiry chap with a cockney accent and a head of fair wavy hair.

The first night's destination was Hluhluwe. This is a large Game Reserve, and the old hunting grounds of Chaka the Zulu King. In recent years it had become just a small railway halt for the local farmers, to get their produce to markets, in surrounding towns. Apart from the local crafts, they grew pine apples which were a good cash crop.

The sweeping panorama of undulating savannah grassland, broken only by small Acacia trees, made this area home, to Lions, Rhino's, Elephants, and Nyala. A Nyala is an antelope with striped markings and twisted spiralling horns. It is much like the Kudu, and the same size as a Waterbuck. The yellowing grass, three feet high, made excellent cover for the hunting big cats. The area was very much, to George, like the top of the Kalahari,

Reception at the Lodge, disbursed the travellers into 'Rondavels' for the night. Round huts, built to look like Original 'Bee-hive' stick and mud homes of the Zulu. Inside, they had air conditioning, mosquito nets, and bed that Chaka would have considered opulent. The top cover, was a 'Kaross', which is a blanket made from Game skins, very traditional.

They had arrived in time, without delay, to go out on an evening trip, with one of the Rangers. It was not considered safe to walk around on one's own, or go in civilian transport, in case of an emergency. This outing was rewarded with some lions at a water hole, and a small herd of Nyala on the other side. A few Giraffe wandered by. but kept going when they saw the Lions. The evenings whet the appetite of the hunters, so the prey is wary.

The ubiquitous zebra were out in force, hundreds of them, like horses in a prairie herd.

At dinner, the main course was a beautifully tender steak of warthog. Very much of the pig family, it tasted a shade richer then pork. What did one expect? Snake and Pigmy pie? George chatted with Tim over a beer and reminisced about London.

Day two was to Swaziland. This was rather a strange diversion for George on his British passport. He was not quite sure how it would be met. In fact there was no problem at all.

Swaziland had been populated by Bushmen until about the 16th Century, when again, Bantu speaking tribes, migrating from the north, pushed them out. The Swazi people had chequered ancestry, but settled under the Zulu banner until the British came along. After battles with the Boers, and later the Red Coats under the Union Flag, in the 1880's Chaka's old Capital became Mbabane. The Country was respected and given Independence in 1968, under it's own Monarchy.

The Hotel had a Casino, which would not be allowed in South Africa, under their strict Religious Laws. In fact this was the prime draw, for holidays and short stays, for Africaaners. There was a trade in prostitution, rumoured, as well. It was not evident or blatantly overt as far as George could see.

George introduced himself to the two single men. They were Doug and Ryan, Canadian Mining Engineers. They were taking time off to explore the sub continent while working on the Gold mines. They were returning to Jo'berg, from Durban, and wanted to see some African Game before going back to Canada. They explained that they don't see much at the bottom of a Mine shaft.

The stay here was brief. The following morning, it was back on the road, and return to S.A. The border checks took a lot longer, than George had anticipated. All bags and suitcases were searched. He asked the driver, why it was so thorough going back into South Africa, than he'd ever seen elsewhere. The driver told him, that the search is for 'Playboy' magazines and pornography, which was available in Swaziland, but not in S.A. The Dutch Reform Church would not tolerate the importation of any of the 'skin' books, so draconian checks at this border were inevitable.

The target today was the Kruger National Park. They were to stay at Skukuza Camp, for the night, and all the next day and night.

There was not a great deal of change in the surroundings, so most of the journey was spent chatting to Doug and Ryan, and letting the world go by, outside.

The accommodation was again based on the hut principle. From the exterior, they resemble a rondavel (a round hut with thatched roof, built of poles). The insides were quite modern. They were equipped with plumbed in showers and ablutions, single beds with Kaross covers, and electric lights. They were spacious and comfortable. The Main Camp was modern, with a large restaurant, festooned with Game Trophy Heads, and Zulu spears and Shields. It had a well tendered bar, which the three single men took full advantage of.

The full day was spent with a guide in a Park's open land rover. Although having been over Wankie, Hluhluhwe, and other National Parks, this was the day George was tosee a leopard. The cat didn't wait around for cameras, or do poses. It was spotted(?) just ahead of the truck lying prone beside the road in the grass. It seemed to be watching some thing on the other side of the road, disturbed it. Up and off he ran, away from them. Admiration from all on the vehicle at seeing such a magnificent specimen.

'Next time I go to a zoo, and see the bored creatures in cages, I know how sorry I will be for them. Having seen them here their natural habitat, I know that this is where they should be'. Ryan said to the other two men.

The leopard was the high-light of the day. Much more Game was seen, so the day was a considerable success for all of them. That evening, those who had never been in the Bush, or experienced seeing such real live animals, were full of glee for the day. City dwellers who only see performing, trained animals, should go on a Safari They should witness themselves, how fabulous these creatures are, when they in their own domain.

The trip to Nelspruit was full of interest scenically. The main road passed some natural views of outstanding features and fall. They stopped and detoured for a look at Lone Creek Falls and the Long Tom Pass. They were back in the Eastern Transvaal, on the northerly heights of the Drakensburg Range. The region was also known as the Crocodile River Mountains.

The Drakensburg Range consists of some of the oldest rock known. Geologists have found rocks over two billion years old there. Some of the caves have evidence of human habitation of the very earliest mankind. The coach tour, cannot stop and absorb all of this, so the journey continued.

Nelspruit is the largest town here, and the Capital of the region. This was the last night out, but spirits were still very high, after all they had seen over the last two days.

The drive from Nelspruit to Johannesburg, was nothing spectacular. Roads and houses and more roads. The two Engineers had their return to work to look forward to, but George had a stay in Jo'berg, and maybe Maxine.

The Bulawayo Travel Agent had found George a pension in the Hillbrow area of Jo'berg. Unbeknown to him then, but later he was aware, that this was the area for transients and travelers.

His first night, he quietly spent having a couple of beers and a Chinese meal. Next morning, a visit from Maine, she had 'looked him up'. Now he had a tour guide of his own, and good company to boot. She was exactly what he wanted in those respects. George hired a car, and they went to inspect the area.

Johannesburg must have been one of the youngest cities in the World. In 1860 it was 'settled' by the Boer Trekkers having been displaced by the British. The Great Trek saw both lines and individual, bullock or ox drawn wagons haul whole families north from the Cape. Just 20 years later, gold was discovered nearby. A gold rush ensued and by 1880, the population had swollen considerably. It created the Witwatersand, which became the biggest gold mining area in Africa. Although one of the most prominent cities of the Country, It was not the Capital.

The main street was called Rissik Street, after a Mr Rissik who went to Britain to secure mining rights. The first Boer War had been from 1880 – 1881, and to the Victor, the ability to give concessions. Here too was the Carlton Centre. At the time it was building phenomena. It had sub ground car-parking area, floors of shops, and offices and apartment in a tower block above.

One day they went to see 'The Cradle of Humankind'. The caves at Skerfontein held incredible memories. Fossils of animals, plants and the first Hominids, dated around 2.6 – 2.8 million years old. The dolomite, limestone caves revealed skulls and bones of 'Australopithecus Africanus'. Not all the caves were open to the public, but what were had a really eerie atmosphere. There are other sites in South Africa where cave paintings indicate the presence of habitation, thousands of years ago.

Another day was spent in Pretoria. The History here, took George back to the Ndabele and Chief Mazilikazi who had been here before he went to Bulawayo. He had gone north, after the Zulu warriors came here back in 1832. In 1855 the Voortrekkers came to settle there. They had their battles with Zulu. One of their leaders Marthinus Pretorius, became the founder of Pretoria. His son was at the Battle of Blood River, which was a resounding victory for the Boers over the Zulu.

The Voortrakker Monument, was not a architectural inspiration, but revered by the Africaaners, for what it represented. It was a Monument to those who died, and those who had the courage and strength to have made the Great Trek. It was the ancestry of the current Africaaners.

The jacaranda lined streets beautified the city, which was the Administrative Capital of South Africa. It was near Pretoria, in a town called Cullinan, that the biggest diamond in the World was discovered.

Back near to Hillbrow was the Stijdom Tower. This Tower was like an enormous Nelson's Column, housing offices and a huge restaurant at the top. The view was spectacular. They could see, from the elevated platforms, what seemed all of Johannesberg.

George was booked on a flight from Jo'berg to Bulawayo. It was time to go back to being a 'Bush Boddy'. He had little money left anyway. He had spent the last 'Rands' that he had on sending postcards to England, and coffees for himself and Maxie at the airport. He gave her his small change. He didn't need it in Rhodesia.

With a tear in her eye, hugs and cuddles, they parted They never saw each other again.

MEMBER IN CHARGE.

Technically speaking, George was still 'attached' to Essexvale. He had only been on secondment to Figtree, On his return to Rhodesia he presented himself, to Benny stone. They shook hands and Benny told him to sit down. His orders were to report to the new Superintendent in Charge of District, at Bulawayo the following day.

The new Superintendent, was non other than his old Chief Inspector at Marandellas, Raymond ware. He told him that Chris Collins had been promoted to Inspector, and transferred to Umtali. In the interim, a young P.O. had been stationed at Figtree, and the place was in a sorry state, administratively. George was to go there as Member-in-Charge, and sort it out.

'You have one month Simpson, to do two months work, not get on out there get started'.

'Right Sir'.

Transport was arranged. George returned to Essexvale. Packed all his stuff and set off for Figtree, again. This directive was in a way creating another first. George would be the first P.O: with less than three years service to be 'Member in Charge of a Section Officers station.

Rafferty O'Flynn was not Irish, he was born and bred Rhodesia. His home was near Mrewa, close to where George had started duty at Marandellas. Rafferty was an exuberant young man, who flailed his arms around when he was describing anything. If he was talking about shooting, his arms would take the pose, and his body with it. He was tall, and slim with brown hair and eyes. He wore spectacles and looked more like a University student than a 'Bush Bobby'.

Rafferty had been stationed at some tiny station on the border, and his move, just after George left, was good for him. However, his idea of the Administration of a Police Station was zero. He had been on his own there for a month, without any help or guidance at all. Chris had been sent to Umtali soon after Rafferty arrived.

Like all Government Organisations, returns have to be done each month. Raff had either not known about them, or done them erroneously. Mr Ware had been correct, two months work in one. The old monthly returns that had been sent had to be re-done, and those not done, had to be done.

There was a petrol issue for the month. As the case that at 'stables', the vehicles are topped up, the figures were all wrong. Was there a case to suspect theft of Govt property? George set about checking all the records.

He discovered that the Sgts had topped up the vehicles each day. Every day the land Rover had ten gallons. The physical dip of the tank showed more than it should have. The issuing officer had put ten in the book column because it was easy to then work out the mileage consumption of the vehicle. It showed that the truck was doing about 5 miles to the gallon, which was ridiculous.

He started by working back on the mileage done, then the average it should have done. Then the physical dip of the tank, and soon re-calculated that the petrol had not been stolen. The truck had not taken ten gallons, or done five miles to the gallon. The Sgt had issued say six gallons, then poured four back into the tank, and recorded ten. Maybe the next day, he had pumped four gallons, and put six back in the tank. Thus the station had not issued thirty gallons a month, although it was in the book, it was still in the deposit. The petrol having been treated to a round trip to the surface and back. The pump recorder confirmed this.

The African police were treated to a morning blasting off shotgun shells, as that monthly record having to be refined, with the number of rounds in stock, and those spent in training over the last two months. Last month's return on this seems to have disappeared(?) when asked for it by radio from Bulawayo.

The old adage 'It is in the post', came to George's rescue a number of times as radio requests for last month's figures were required. It meant long days and working every weekend to clear it all. After a couple of weeks it was done.

Although Raff and George shared the single men's bungalow, there was no 'let-up' on him to help clear up his mess. Both being single, they managed a few evenings down at the Hotel together to break the sole view of the Police Camp. Luckily they timed the evenings, to coincide when the farmers were in town, so they had pleasant drinking bouts with the Barbers or Jim.

George also arranged 'Training days' with all the Police Reservists that could make it. Those days were great fun. The meals were taken at the Hotel, and if any could stay back after the Training, a bit of 'Hospitality'.

George sent Raff out a few times on short Patrols, but kept him away from Solusi Mission for the time being. He got on really well with the staff at the Cyrene Mission. Two Europeans ran it. The Principle was

Dorothy Banks who was a founder of the Rhodesia 'Aloe and Succulents' Society. She was an authority on such matters. She was a small lady with greying hair in a bun. Studious looking, she wore glasses, and had a prim appearance, but she could be fun. She had a sharp and intelligent sense Of humour. Her Assistant was a large unkempt looking chap called Marty Walcott. This first impression of him belied a good mind, and dry wit.

Cyrene was more Of a school than a Mission, though religious instruction was part of the curriculum. It had well kept gardens and was in its own grounds. The Schoolrooms were in a single white block building with a corrugated steel roof. A bungalow nearby provided living quarters for Dorothy and Marty, and there was much speculation as to their relationship. However. no one really cared or asked personnel questions.

A radio message from Selukwe one-day, brought George's mind back to his days at Nvamapanda. Moyo (l) was not fulfilling his libolo obligations to his wife's father. The man had gone into Selukwe and threatened Tribal action if this was not remedied. The matter was considered important enough for action. It was not considered true to the dignity of the Force, to have its members hauled before a Chief on such an allegation.

Geroge had Moyo brought before him and gave him a stern ticking off. He then sent Moyo out on a patrol, on the understanding that his extra patrol pay would be sent direct to Selukwe for libolo payment. This was not to happen again.

Moyo (2) was a tall, but well proportioned young man. He was much more taciturn than his namesake. He was studying his 'O' levels in the evenings. He had the same biology book that George had studied with when he had done his, some years before. On a few occasions after that, George spent time with him, talking about the blood system and other anatomical subjects.

Daily routines kept everyone busy enough. a quiet day came along, George would invent jobs like tidying the Camp. One such day was to turn out more exciting, as it was discovered that there was a snakes nest under the parade square. Petrol was poured at the slightly built up side and the grit parade square set on fire.

George had a visit one day from Hansie de Villiers the old Africaaner who's cow had the breach birth. He came up to the Camp, with a jar of pickled fish. He had a chat, and went on his way. When he and Raff tried the fish, George wasn't so keen on it. It all got eaten though, mostly by 'Pencil'.

Being Member In Charge, meant that he was also Public Prosecutor for the area. When such occasions demanded, they converted Chris' old bungalow lounge, into a Court room. The P.P. had to 'book' the services of a circuit Magistrate in advance. Most of the occasions when these were required, came from Sgt. Dude caught Africans on the train, whom it transpired were fugitives, and had to be formally remanded. This was all simple enough. The Magistrate would then have lunch with George and depart.

One Court day, George also had a case where the driver of a car, who was not the owner, was caught driving without a licence. The owner was also charged with allowing this to happen. The driver was guilty and fined. The owner however was discharged over a legality George, without specialised legal knowledge was a bit taken aback, but never the less, after Court, lunch was taken. The Magistrate and George had always got on quite well, and this was not to change. The matter was discussed over a bowl of soup, and was rather instruction for George, who was happy to learn.

A Senior Officer was to visit the Station. This was normal, in that they made Officers visits to all the Stations from time to time. Elbe camp was tidied up, even to re painting the white stones up the driveway. Hedges trimmed, grass cut back, every thing was spot on. Rafferty was to get the A.P. to do a small honour guard.

The Senior Officer that came, was the father of the national service P.O. that put a dead snake in the 'fridge at Dett. Superintendent Dickens arrived while George was attending to an incoming radio message. He made his way into the M.I.C.'s office and made himself at home. Tea was called for. Dickens was happy about the state of the place and the work George had done.

The meeting ended very cordially, especially after a reasoned discussion about the role of experienced and senior African Sergeants, becoming ranked higher than junior P.O.s. The whole subject had merit, and was notable, for the fact that it was being considered, putting an African above a European in rank.

The radio message that had come in, was from Dett. It was George's old pal Graham, who told him that 'Pencil's' family had no money, Some time ago, George had wanted to open a savings account for 'Pencil' but it hadn't been pursued. Now it was 'Pencil's' turn to be dressed down. George wondered afterwards if he was to poisoned for it.

A difficult case came into the Camp. Gunter Cronje was an Africaaner who had a small farm towards Marula. One of his African labourers had stupidly thrown away a Cigarette butt, which was still lit. The butt had started to burn some grass and eventually a small paddock had been lost. Cronje had cattle, so the loss of so much grass was very important to him. He would have to rent some land off a neighbour as and when he would need to. It would cost him quite a bit of money.

The labourcr had been brought to the station by Cronje. and had admitted what he had done. The plum that landed in George's lap, was that Cronje wanted the lad punished.

Unravelling the whole picture was not straightforward. As the pieces of the picture were disclosed. It was more of a wrangle than at first seemed.

Cronje wanted to keep the lad as he was a good worker. He did not want to have to train another to take his place. He could charge him with all kinds of damage to property. There were numerous possibilities with relevant sections and acts. To George there was no point in having him sent to prison, which would happen if he couldn't pay a fine. The lad had no money to pay a fine. Farm workers the world over get poor wages, but are kept for their services in food and quarters.

George told Sgt Chivero to take the truck and get the lad's father or uncle or some relative, who was an adult. 'This may take some time Mr Cronje, do you want to leave the lad here and pop back later?' While Cronje had gone, George set about doing other things. It would take time for Chivero to do his task.

Later that day, Sgt Chivero returned with an uncle. The whole allegation was put to his uncle, who also was a farm worker, with no money. Cronje returned and so George decided what he was going to do. Provided he had the full co-operation from all parties the matter could be dealt with.

Speaking to each in turn he asked the following questions.

'Mr Cronje, if the lad is punished, will you have him back to work for you?' 'Yes 1 will'.

'But you want the lad punished for his stupidity?' 'That's right'.

This was interpreted for the lad and the uncle, by Chivero.

'Do you admit your mistake and stupid behaviour?'

Answering through Sgt Chivero, he glumly admitted it all.

'Do you understand, if I take you to Court, you may be jailed, or made to pay a fine. If you cannot pay the fine, you may go to jail because of that'.

Again through Sgt Chivero the lad understand that his future was looking very grim indeed.

'With your uncles permission, and with Mr Cronje and your uncle as witnesses, I am offering you a choice. If you accept my punishment, you will keep your job, You will not be fined or go to jail. Will you accept my punishment?'

Looking rather fearful, but comprehending his options, he nodded and mumbled acceptance. As did the uncle.

'Right Sergeant, go and get a stick, suitable for giving the lad a caning'.

Sgt Chivero came back a quarter hour later, with a flexible yard long stick without knots or barbs of any kind.

So, with the uncle and Mr Cronje as witnesses, George had the lad bear his backside over his desk. Sgt Chivero gave him a good old-fashioned six of the best. It made the lad wince, but no skin was broken, just welts. The same that school children used to get to keep them in line.

Mr Cronje was happy, he had his labourer back after being punished. The uncle was content that he hadn't been punished, by having to pay a fine for his nephew. He was also relieved he didn't have to get a caning for him too.

Who could tell if the boy was happy. He was smarting from his wounds, but he had a job, and he was not going to prison.

No crime was ever recorded.

It was one of those weeks, when things just didn't fit in to place cleanly. On the Monday, a meeting was to take place, which required the M.I.C. as his position in the Community required it. The meeting was about new farming legislation and was to be chaired by some one from the D.C.'s Office. As expected, it turned out to be very boring for George. He didn't have long to go' before his three years were up. He had had a letter from his mother to say that his father was ill. His chest was not so good, and his blood circulation poor. So that was it, he was going back to England at the end of his contract.

To make that week worse, the following night, George and Raff were roused by the night duty Constable. A goods train going from Bulawayo through to Botswana had been pilfered. The Signalman at Marula had noticed ripped tarpaulins over the backs of open trucks.

Raff was deployed to take some men and search the side of the tracks from Cyrene, back to Figtree. George would take a team, down to Marula take a statement from the Signalman and work back.

Thus it was, the whole night was spent walking alongside sections of railway line, looking for evidence. They came across some pairs of plimsolls which had been thrown from the trucks. Why on earth were they transporting boxes of plimsolls in an open truck, covered only be a tarpaulin, He could not imagine. Perhaps they were export only plimsolls.

The Railway Police took over the investigation. It seemed that crooks will canvass the marshalling yards in Bulawayo. They jump on a train with any sort of cargo they think worth stealing. This time they chose a cargo, of low quality plimsolls coming through Figtree. The whole night was lost. Now he had Rafferty to get up in the morning though.

George's farewell was made into a party for all. Telephone calls to all the farmers, and Cyrene Mission. It was Dorothy and Marty who gave him a waistcoat with a front of real elephant skin as a farewell gift. Maybe a beer mug would have an engraving of a stick over a plimsoll.

George was to go to Bulawayo, hand back and sign in, all his Government issue uniforms, belts and hats etc. Once that was done, the Contract had been fully filled, and he was free to go. He was offered a new three year contract, but with his father being ill, he would not accept the tie.

He has been in touch with Penny in Salisbury. He planned to take the plane from Bulawayo to Salisbury, spend a few days there, then fly back to the U.K. He had with him, just the clothes he had carried over from England, and one extra pair of shoes, the Game skin ones, and a tanned kudu skin. His other baggage, was a thousand memories, and a bunch of photos.

He landed in Salisbury and was met by Penny, and taken to her family home.

The whole family were glad to see him, but sad that he was leaving for England. They understood that it was because of his father, but the emotions were mixed. The evening was spent with dinner and endless speculation about all their futures. Que Sera.

Penny took him to the airport, to see him off. She took him to check-in and they had their last hugs and kisses

At the airport it was declared, that his luggage was overweight. He hadn't the money pay for excess baggage, so he took out the kudu skin, and gave it to Penny.

It was over. Three years in Africa. The sights and sounds of the dark Continent will always be with him. One thing about experience, Governments can't tax you on them.

George Shipman came from a respectable middle class family. However, he found his life unfulfilling, and wanted to travel and explore new things.

Circumtances had spoiled his chances of a higher education, although he had the intelligence to go further than he did.

Whenever opportunities arose, instead of remaining in his life's certainties and comforts, he took the chances that opened to him. The doors of life for him, led from working on Oil-Rigs, to Africa. He found his way, spending three years, in a totally new world, much more than he could have imagined.

From one side of the Country to another, in the then, Rhodesia, he experienced responsibility, sights and deeds, now dwindling to extinction in this modern world.